BRINGING CHRIST BACK

BRINGING CHRIST BACK

Robert Nash, S.J.

Our Sunday Visitor, Inc.
Huntington, Indiana 46750

Imprimi Potest:
De Licentia Superiorum Ordinis: Patritius Doyle
Praep. Prov. Hib. Soc. Jesu
July 7, 1977

Nihil Obstat:
Hilary Lawton, S.J.
Censor Deputatus

Imprimatur:
✝Dermot Ryan, D.D.
Archbishop of Dublin
April 7, 1978

ISBN: 0-87973-642-9
Library of Congress Catalog Number: 78-69992

Cover design by Clete Olinger

Published, printed and bound in the U.S.A. by
Our Sunday Visitor, Inc.
Noll Plaza
Huntington, Indiana 46750

642

DEDICATION

Dedicated to Our Lady of Sorrows

For my esteemed friend Mary Murphy, who for forty years has been hanging with Christ on the cross.

ACKNOWLEDGMENTS

Both for inspiration and content, I am indebted to many in the production of this book, but space allows me to mention just a few.

For nearly all Scripture quotations I have used St. Jerome's Latin Vulgate, often in a slightly modernized version of the Douay-Rheims English translation, but in some twenty key passages I have quoted brief excerpts from The Jerusalem Bible, originally published by Les Editions du Cerf, Paris, with English translation copyright © 1966, 1967 and 1968 by Darton, Longman & Todd Ltd, London, and Doubleday & Company, Inc., New York. All rights reserved.

In two or three important sections I have used extracts from *Songs in the Night* by a Poor Clare Colettine, copyright © 1936 by Sheed & Ward, 31 Paternoster Row, London, E.C.4. It is no longer in print, but you may be able to find a copy in your parish or diocesan library.

Acknowledgment is also extended to the following, from whom permission has been received:

To Macmillan Publishing Co., Inc., New York, and Weidenfeld & Nicolson Ltd, London, for an excerpt from *Memoirs* by Jozsef Cardinal Mindszenty (English translation copyright ©1974 by Macmillan Publishing Co., Inc. All rights reserved).

To Ave Maria Press, Notre Dame, Ind., and Collins Publishers, London, for excerpts from *Poustinia: Christian Spirituality of the East for Western Man* by Catherine de Hueck Doherty, copyright © 1975 by Ave Maria Press. All rights reserved.

Also to Ave Maria Press for an excerpt from *Words in Pain*

I have quoted the prose and poetry of Msgr. Robert Hugh Benson, Elizabeth Barrett Browning, Father Frederick Faber, Caryll Houselander, John Cardinal Newman, etc., as well as Shakespeare, Tennyson and Wordsworth, but perhaps the most valuable aid to determining the mind of Christ outside the Bible — more valuable perhaps than the writings of St. Augustine, St. Francis de Sales, St. Ignatius, St. John of the Cross, St. Thomas Aquinas, etc., contained herein — is *The Imitation of Christ* by Thomas à Kempis. I can recommend a rendering in modern English by Father Albert J. Nevins, M.M., copyright © 1973 by Our Sunday Visitor, Inc. All rights reserved.

Finally, to bring home the Passion of Christ in His members, I have cited the lives of several modern saints and almost-saints: St. Maria Goretti, Blessed Maximilian Kolbe, O.F.M. Conv., Edel Quinn, St. John Vianney, Ven. Matt Talbot, Mother Teresa of Calcutta, St. Thérèse of Lisieux, etc. Excellent biographies are available on most of these (e.g., on Mother Teresa, *Love Without Boundaries* or Muggeridge's *Something Beautiful for God* published by Our Sunday Visitor and Harper & Row respectively; on Talbot, books by Sir Joseph Glynn and several others), but for nearly all of them in outline, including the children of Fatima, read *Saints & Heroes Speak* by Father Robert J. Fox, copyright © 1977 by Our Sunday Visitor, Inc. All rights reserved.

Robert Nash, S.J.
Pentecost, 1978

CONTENTS

RAISING THE CURTAIN

RAISING THE CURTAIN

We were sitting at a meal, a group of about thirty Jesuits. Lent was coming in two or three weeks. "At this time every year," said the priest on my right, "I take the Passion of Christ for the subject of my mental prayer. My idea is to work through it quietly day by day and finish up with the Resurrection at Easter. But I have never succeeded. The subject is vast, inexhaustible. Every detail, indeed almost every phrase is so meaningful, that it seems to open out wide vistas providing endless material for reflection and prayer."

I understood and agreed. The Passion is a love story that holds one enthralled. It is written in a language intelligible to every true lover, the language of sacrifice. It is written in red, the red ink of the blood of Jesus Christ. It has one special feature that makes it peculiarly attractive. Unlike other romances we may perhaps have read, this one is fact, not fiction. It is the sheer, unadorned, unadulterated truth. It all actually happened. It is happening still. It concerns me so intimately and personally that I can truly say that the entire Passion of the Son of God was suffered for my sake.

It belongs to me completely. The fruits of the Passion would not be more fully mine if all the millions of men were to be deprived of them and they were all given to me for my exclusive possession. This is so because in the Passion we have a love that is infinite. The principal actor in the drama is an omnipotent lover. Throughout, this lover is, so to say, taxing the powers of his omnipotence by pouring out, without stint or measure, love and grace on each single individual, the only limitation being that individual's capacity to receive. St. Paul would seem to be stunned when, with his mind flooded with the light of the Holy Spirit, he looked and saw and recognized this breathtaking truth. One can stand close to him and watch this man rising from his knees, clapping his right hand to his forehead and, in a transport of joy, exclaiming: "The Son of God . . . loved *me* and delivered himself *for me*" (Galatians 2:20).

The Good News

Suppose I am living in Dublin and my mother, whom I love dearly, is lying seriously ill in a hospital in San Francisco. She is due to have a critical operation at ten o'clock in the morning. The surgeon has promised to phone me at five this afternoon and give me a report. I am there well ahead of time, seated in the phone booth, anxiously waiting. After what seems an age, at last the call comes through. I lift the receiver, hold it to my right ear and listen. "Hello, Father," says a cheerful voice. "This is Doctor X. from San Francisco. This is one of the most pleasant messages I have ever had to give. I cannot say how happy I am to be able to tell you that your dear mother's operation has proved to be a complete success. We found after all that her condition was not as serious as we feared. At the moment she is sleeping peacefully. We think she should be sitting up in ten days or so and be ready to make the trip back to Ireland in another week after that."

My reactions as I hang up the phone? Instinctively I murmur a fervent "Thanks be to God!" A ton weight has been lifted off my heart. I want to tell the world the good news. Stepping out of the telephone booth, I meet a man on the street, a total stranger. I hold him up and tell him my story. I cannot keep it to myself. Everyone must know.

The Passion is good news, *the* good news. The first people to write about it were the four evangelists. Since then, saints and scholars by the thousand have pored over the sacred text, examining and comparing different manuscripts, praying for the light of truth and the warmth of love. They experience an insatiable craving to tell the world what they have found. They seize the pen, covering page after page and piling volume upon volume in the effort to put into words what they know by conviction. This love story is true! "Jesus Christ loved *me* and delivered Himself up *for me.*" Immense libraries have been built all over the world to house the vast output of literature this has inspired. Are the authors satisfied that they have got the message across? Not at all. The task is hopeless; they throw down their pens in despair. Is there a man, or even an angel, endowed with the gift of a language capable of expressing the love of Jesus Christ in His Passion? "There are many other things that Jesus did. If all were written down, the world itself, I think, would not hold all the books that would have to be written" (John 21:25).

Relevant Still

Why, then, write another book on the same theme? Not indeed because the author in this case imagines himself to have any charism or exceptional competence, but because he feels quite certain that one of the most pressing needs of the world of the Seventies and Eighties is a vivid realization, built on divine faith, that the Passion is true, that it will furnish us with the key to many of our problems. "All we, like sheep, have gone astray. Everyone has turned aside into his own path" (Isaiah 53:6). We exist in a period of lostness. By and large we have lost our sense of the supernatural. Many of us suffer from remorse or nostalgia for the past, disillusionment and cynicism about the present, and fear and foreboding and insecurity as we try to pierce the veil that covers the unknown future. Let it be stated with all the emphasis we can command that Christ is the answer; that there is chaos all around because Christ has been lost; that in the Passion, meditated upon prayerfully and perseveringly, we shall find light in our darkness and courage to keep going on. That explains why we have given this book the title *BRINGING CHRIST BACK*.

A good friend of mine was hesitant about encouraging me to write it. The Stations of the Cross, I was assured, are now "out," and stress on the Passion has been played down since Vatican II. One sickens of so many such irresponsible, irrational statements. Many of our excellent laity are bewildered by them, especially when they have to listen to them being solemnly propounded by priests who are ordained to preach the gospel. "We will have none of the reticence of those who are ashamed," writes St. Paul, "no deceitfulness or watering down the word of God. The way we commend ourselves to every human being with a conscience is by stating the truth openly in the sight of God" (2 Corinthians 4:2).

So I embark on my self-imposed task, confident that the Holy Spirit will shed light on the printed word; that He will convince us there never was a time when the right attitude toward the Passion was more urgently needed, for individuals and nations.

Solzhenitsyn

I quote from a letter lying open before me on my desk as I type. "At present I am reading Alexander Solzhenitsyn's *The Gulag Archipelago*. My reaction to the first few chapters is that Christ never suffered like this. His Passion, appalling indeed though it was, was all over and done with in a matter of less than twenty-four hours, whereas the tortures described by Solzhenitsyn dragged on interminably for weeks and months and even longer. The unfortunate victims had no idea of the length of time during which they would have to carry on. They realized in many cases that only death would bring them relief.

"Further, the book tells of dreadful atrocities Christ did not have to bear. Some of those who suffered, for instance, had their eyes gouged out. I'm sure there is something gone wrong with my thinking here. I feel that Christ must somehow have packed into those few hours a quantity of suffering far in excess of what all men of all time have borne. I very much want to believe this, but I don't see the answer to the question it raises. Perhaps you can throw light on it for me, Father. I shall be very grateful."

Well, we can try. We can state confidently that Christ, in a general way, did probably suffer more than all the rest of mankind combined. But this is obviously not true of His physical pains. Many others suffered in their bodies for whole years, sometimes for a whole lifetime. It is also true that Christ did not go through all the different kinds of suffering inflicted on some of those men and women who followed Him so closely on the road to Calvary. In spite of this it remains at least probable that His sufferings were far in excess of anything the rest of us have ever been called upon to endure. We suggest two reasons why this would seem to be so, keeping in mind that we are considering here only His mental sufferings.

First of all let it be said that different people have different capacities for bearing pain, depending largely on the condition of their bodies. A farmer, accustomed all his life to working on the land, out in all weathers, has become in large measure almost impervious to the changes of climate. He makes light of the bitter winds blowing from the east and he will talk about a veritable deluge as a healthy "drop of rain"! To another who has lived an indoor life, sheltered in the comfort of a well-heated home, the cold will be agony. He is more sensitive to its attack.

Or take a chronic invalid who for years has lived on a bed of sickness and has learned, in the hard school of experience, how to bear it with patience. (And how many of these noble examples start up in one's mind!) Now compare with this sufferer a man who has enjoyed excellent health all his life and who has to be rushed to hospital this evening as a result of a head-on car crash. Once the immediate grave danger has passed, he tends to become restless and demanding and given to complaining, though actually there are several others in the same ward who have more to put up with but manage to smile through.

Now the body of Christ was expressly fashioned in order that it might be sensitive to pain to a degree beyond which it would be impossible for unaided human nature to go. It has even been suggested that He would have died before He reached Calvary — during the scourging at the pillar, for example — had he not sustained His life by a miracle. There are difficulties in the way of such a supposition, but it does remain at least plausible. The spectacle presented by this accumulation of sufferings is most movingly described by the prophet. He sees the suffering servant as "without beauty, without majesty . . . no looks to attract our eyes; an object despised and rejected by men; a man of sorrows and familiar with suffering. . . . Ours were the sufferings that he bore, ours the sorrows that he carried. . . . He was pierced through for our faults, crushed for our sins . . . for our faults struck down in death. . . . From the crown of the head to the soles of the feet there is not a sound spot: bruises and wounds and swelling sores, not dressed, not bandaged, nor soothed with oil . . ." (Isaiah 53:2-8; 1:6). If now we turn to what He suffered in His soul we shall see even more clearly that here, especially, what He had to endure surpassed immeasurably the anguish and torment of mind that all of us combined have to bear. He was in the fullest sense a real man, like us in everything except sin. Thus, while remaining God, He took from the Virgin Mary a body of flesh and, by what He suffered in soul and body, atoned superabundantly for our sins. What makes our pain such a trial is that we cannot keep our thoughts off it if we see it is going to come, and once it has come, each new moment is added on to the moments that have gone before. If I could forget all that has preceded and focus my thoughts on only the one present moment of suffering at any time, my feeling of pain would lessen enormously.

Brutes feel far less pain than we do because they cannot reflect on what causes it, nor add together the sum total of all that has gone before, to which must now be added the present. They do not know that they exist; each moment as it passes is their all, lived in complete isolation from past or future. "It is the intellectual comprehension of pain," writes Newman, "as a whole, going through successive moments, which gives it its special power and keenness, and it is the soul only, which brutes do not have, which is capable of that comprehension."

Applying this to Our Lord, we can see that He was going through His Passion, not only on Good Friday but throughout His whole life. "I have great sadness and continual sorrow," wrote Paul (Romans 9:2). Caryll Houselander wrote that "Christ endured the entire Passion for full thirty-three years." This opinion is advanced by those who say that not only His physical sufferings but the sufferings of His mind, too, exceeded what all others put together endured. What makes our pain of mind so severe is that we cannot dissociate any moment of it from what has gone before and what is still to follow. I cannot rid myself of thoughts about the critical operation I have to face on Wednesday. I suffer much by anticipation. And if, having worked myself up to expecting it on Wednesday, I am now told it must inevitably be deferred for a week, my suffering is increased still more. Similarly, when the ordeal is over I keep going back on it in my thoughts, describing every detail of it to friends who visit me.

There are those who think that Christ had some sort of experience similar to this. If He did, it would help to explain how much greater were His sufferings than ours. To show how continually the thought of His future agony was in His mind, some quote the warning He gave His apostles. "Taking the Twelve aside he said to them: 'Now we are going up to Jerusalem and everything that is written by the prophets about the Son of Man is to come true. For he will be handed over to the pagans and will be mocked, maltreated and spat upon, and when they have scourged him they will put him to death, and on the third day he will rise again'" (Luke 18:31-33). Others deny the value of this evidence. They maintain that what we know about Our Lord, and Our Lady too for that matter, was that they concentrated on what has been aptly called "the sacrament of the present moment." Christ lived fully in the present, lovingly subjecting Himself to what He knew to be the Father's will in the here and now. He recommended us to take no thought for tomorrow, and in this His own practice was in complete harmony with His theory. To dwell excessively on one's own pains and aches, to elaborate on them for anyone willing to listen, is no mark of virtue. Such an attitude betrays a subtle, though probably unsuspected, desire for an adulation to flatter self-love. Christ was a perfect man, like us in everything except sin. So He would have been content to meet each day and each circumstance as it came to Him from the hand of His heavenly Father.

We have thus put forward two views, one saying that Christ endured the Passion for thirty-three years, the other maintaining that He concentrated only on the immediate present. Both sides are concerned to present us with a Christ who loved us and delivered Himself for us.

Extravagance?

Because Jesus Christ is God, His every action is infinite in value. Hence, had the work of our redemption been differently planned He might have freed us from our sins without suffering. He might, for instance, have come into this world as a full-grown man instead of coming as a helpless little baby. He might have lived among us, not for thirty-three years, but only for one hour, or even for only a minute. During that brief earthly sojourn He might have offered on our behalf a single sigh from His Sacred Heart or a drop of His blood, one tear or one short prayer, one cry to His Father to forgive us.

Any one of these gestures or petitions would have been sufficient to redeem this world from its sin a thousand times over. "One drop of His blood," writes St. Thomas Aquinas, "would have been enough to save the whole world from every sin." That tiny act of the God-Man would have far surpassed in value all the penances and prayers of all the saints, from the first moment of time till the last. It would have to be placed on a pedestal all its own, in its own special category. Consider the deeds of holy men and women, from the dawn of creation till the day of judgment; pass in review their prolonged fastings, their hours of persevering prayer and vigil, their incessant journeys — often on foot and without shoes — made under blazing suns or in face of icy winds and rain and blinding snowstorms, gladly undertaken for the one, only purpose of bringing God to souls and souls to God. Think of the persecutions to which they stood up, the tyrants they defied, their deaths in the amphitheater where they were torn into pieces by wild beasts. Witness the horrors of the concentration camps of our own day and the satanic devices used to make men suffer.

As to the value of all this testifying to the love of Christ, the Church leaves us in no state of doubt. It has officially declared, in thousands of cases, that this "cloud of witnesses" has practiced Christian virtue to a heroic degree, and over a lengthy period, as a result of which they are now certainly in heaven. But it still remains true that all they did or refused to do, because of their loyalty to Christ, has a finite, limited value only. Whether this be collectively considered or regarded as each one's special contribution to the whole, it could never be sufficient to atone for sin.

But Jesus Christ is God. His tiniest act, therefore, has an altogether unique value. It is endless, stretching out limitlessly beyond the confines of time, transcending the powers of all human calculations to measure. Put that one short prayer of Christ, or that drop of blood, into one pan of a balance. In the other pan pile up all the prayers and penances and sacrifices of the saints of all time, including even those of Mary, His blessed mother. The pan bearing Christ's tiny act sinks down, outweighing all the rest. We are dealing here with things incommensurable, in totally different spheres. It is something like trying to compare the light of the sun with the speed at which a car is traveling.

All this is being directed to a point at which we have now arrived. If one moment of Christ's prayer was infinite in value, what must be the long hours during which He prayed in the desert, or the entire nights during which He knelt on the mountainside? If one drop of His blood, the blood of the God-Man, possesses a value that baffles the powers of human language to tell, what then are we to say about the blood that soaked His clothes in Gethsemane, the blood issuing from so many wounds inflicted on His body during the scourging at the pillar, the blood drained to its last drop on the cross and offered for the salvation of the world? Two excellent priests told me recently, independently of each other, that they believed nobody would go to hell! I admit that this startled me, and I feel bound to be slow in accepting it. But as I was writing the last few paragraphs about the value of Christ's sufferings, I began to think that perhaps the theory was not so fantastic after all. Certainly one could at least say that Christ will leave nothing undone to save every soul — short of forcing one's free will.

We would have infinite, inexhaustible treasure to draw from had Christ offered one insignificant act for our salvation. What words can we find, then, to express what actually did happen? We are tempted to employ a phrase that doesn't make sense and say that we have an infinite number of infinities put at our disposal! This is why we headed this section "Extravagance?"

Love Is the Answer

Indeed it might be argued, in view of what we have been saying, that our Redeemer is wasteful of His gifts. Why all this lavish outpouring of blood and all this accumulation of sufferings when He could have saved us just as well in the easy way? It is true that if He had chosen the easy way He would have abundantly satisfied the demands of justice. Our sins would have been forgiven and the way to heaven opened to us once more. For that, of course, eternity would have been too short to thank Him. But let us not forget what we said on the first page — that the Passion is the most marvelous love story ever told. Now whereas justice remains satisfied when its strict demands have been met, love is always breaking down its banks and expanding all the time. Love never thinks it has done enough. Love knows no rest as long as anything remains ungiven.

That is why the psalmist cries out that ours is indeed a most generous, superabundant redemption (Psalm 130) in which Christ takes away the sins of the world. It is also the reason why St. Luke talks about "good measure, pressed down, shaken together, and flowing over" (Luke 6:38). We think that St. John is even more forthright when he tells us that the giving of God is regardless of any measuring out at all. We bless St. Paul for assuring us that "in all things we are made rich in him . . . so that nothing is wanting to us in any grace . . ." and why, from another context, we cry out with the same apostle: "Thanks be to God for his unspeakable gift" (2 Corinthians 9:15).

In this opening chapter we are simply raising the curtain for the drama to be acted out on the stage before us. We are keeping the lights turned full on Him who is the central character from beginning to end. All others have a secondary place. Some love Him dearly and share intimately in His sufferings. Others conspire against Him and leave nothing undone to bring about His death and crucifixion. Many merely look at Calvary and pass by, uninterested. All these will come out from the wings in due course.

As for ourselves, we cannot remain mere passive spectators. We have to absorb into our minds and hearts the truth presented to us, to share actively with Christ in it, feeling what He feels, so that our own lives become a prolongation of His Passion, reaching all the distance from Calvary to our Eighties. We are being

invited to go to school again. The doctrine is sublime. The teacher brings to His task "the power of God and the wisdom of
God." Throughout, we shall find in Him a sweet persuasiveness,
for He will ask us to do nothing He has not done already Himself. "Jesus began to do and to teach." His practice is always consistent with His theory.

Our Title

BRINGING CHRIST BACK is a humble effort to help spread
the good news. The late Cardinal Jean Danielou talked about an
"implacable urgency" to share it, especially with the vast
numbers of pagans who have never even heard the name of
Christ. But why concern ourselves with these, asked the cardinal,
seeing that they can save their souls without their being visible
members of the Catholic Church? "This problem," he replied,
"is based on incorrect premises. The source of the apostolic life is
not necessity, but *the exigency of love.* It is not merely the question
of souls to be moved but the love of God that leads us to want
Him to be known and loved; the pain we feel as often as we
remember what these poor souls, through no fault of their own,
are missing. We desire to bring Christ to souls and we desire to
bring souls to Christ. Too often we think only of the first. The
apostolic spirit, flowing from the love of Christ, takes on an implacable urgency."

We hope that these words of the cardinal may indicate our
reason for putting these pages together. It is our experience that
the written word has a way of seeping into all sorts of places and
falling into the hands of all sorts of persons. If these pages encouraged not only priests and religious but our laity also —
indeed our laity most of all — to enter with zest on the gigantic
task of BRINGING CHRIST BACK, we could very well find
ourselves meeting with a success that might seem almost miraculous. At this point a question suggests itself: Why are so many of

us unmoved in the face of the miracle of God's love for us as shown in the Passion of Christ? The saints were simply swept off their feet with amazement and gratitude and joy as often as they thought along these lines. They were seized upon by one over-mastering longing — to spread the good news, to convince the world of what they knew from personal experience to be the truth. Everything else in their lives dwindled to the vanishing point. Have we to admit that while we admire them, our admiration is from a respectable distance? We feel little, if any, of their burning zeal. If the truth were known, perhaps we would have to say we were somewhat bored by their effervescent enthusiasm. On the whole we are willing enough to let them go their way and ask only to be allowed to go ours.

Why is this? Why can we be gripped by a good novel or TV show that is all fiction and remain unmoved by the story, the true story, of the divine romance? Why do we feel sympathy for the hero who never existed outside the fertile imagination of the author and be so callous before the indomitable courage of the real, living Christ?

The Passion will have its full effect in the measure in which we refuse to tolerate selfishness in our lives. "If every year," says Thomas à Kempis, "we rooted out one fault we would soon become perfect men." Father Karl Rahner has drawn up a long list of the defects we easily condone. These constitute a barrier to grace and leave us largely insensible to the appeal of the Passion. Here are some of them: "Impatience, coarseness, talkativeness; laughing at the faults of others; egoism in everyday life; waste of time; moral cowardice; stubbornness, moodiness, disorder in work; postponement of the unpleasant; gossip, conceit, self-praise; the tendency to talk too much about oneself, and so forth. . . ."

Christ says: "Blessed are the clean of heart, for they shall see God" (Matthew 5:8). This by no means applies to cleansing from only grave sin. As long as we habitually condone any defects like those on Rahner's list we shall never have more than a superficial appreciation of the power of the Passion of Christ. We shall give to it, as Newman would say, a "notional" assent, not a "real" assent. Without this effort at purity of heart, seriously undertaken, even our reception of the sacraments and our prayers will fall short of producing their full effect.

Says the French Jesuit Père Rigoleu: "One single unmortified passion, one deliberate imperfection with which we are unwilling to part, one imperfect habit, which we are neglecting to correct, may be enough to retain a soul for years, yes, even for a whole lifetime, lingering on the threshold of the most perfect state — union with God — into which He would have introduced it had this particular impediment been removed."

As we watch the drama unfold itself before our eyes, it is of the first importance to keep remembering that Christ is a real man, not merely God who is assuming the ways and appearance of man, but a man in as literal a sense as John Smith or Tom Ryan. Commenting on Karl Adam's fine book *Christ Our Brother*, the translator says: "Convinced that dogma is the very structure of the Christian life and that any dimming of dogma is bound to impair that life, Dr. Adam would have us meditate on the doctrinal fact that Our Lord is not only true God but also true and perfect man. . . . He hopes that by a better knowledge of 'the firstborn of many brothers,' we may all be drawn into closer and more confident relations with him, and with our brethren through him."

The Passion is a challenge. If God has loved us to this extent, St. John insists, then we must love each other. There is a fair amount of talk today about love and loving, about care and caring. It is a happy sign. It would be disastrous if this love were to degenerate into mere humanistic philanthropy, into a kindness and sympathy that would be the expression of a mere natural reaction. Genuine Christian love does not at all frown on natural compassion but raises it to the level of a supernatural motive. This means that we love all men because Christ loved them, because He assures us that what we do to them is done to Himself. Christian love recognizes *Him* in the recipient of its gifts. The cross is thus not only the symbol of Christ's sufferings. It is also His pulpit. He spoke from the cross on Good Friday, and after twenty centuries His words are still "alive and active. They can judge the secret thoughts and emotions of men." The summary of these words comes from St. John who was standing by that pulpit on the day Christ died. "My dearest," he writes, "if God has so loved us, then we ought also to love one another." (1 John 4:11.)

The Problem of Pain

There is one more preliminary to be touched upon before we embark on the story itself. That is the problem of pain. The world all around us is full of sorrow. Nothing would be easier than to expand that statement. We know about it from our own experience in this valley of tears, and to forestall any chance lest we might forget, the media pursue us all day and every day, all night and every night, serving up to us all the harrowing details and almost compelling us to look and learn.

The picture, admittedly, is often grim. It is overcast with dark clouds. The atmosphere is charged with woeful forebodings. But for the man of faith the sunlight keeps bursting in through the clouds, and no groans or lamentations can quite drown the thrilling assurance that comes across: "He loved me and delivered himself for me." With that truth rooted deep in our minds and hearts, we are moved to lift up our voices in song, despite the miseries surrounding us. Three young men were flung in a furnace of fire by the order of a cruel tyrant. God protected them. The flames left them uninjured. They sang, with joyousness in their hearts and the hymn that arose from them is one of the Church's precious possessions to this day. You will find it in the third chapter of the prophet Daniel, beginning with the fifty-seventh verse. No song or prayer could be more relevant for us as we survive the holocausts in the Seventies and Eighties.

Far be it from us to suggest that we are indifferent to the sufferings of others, or that we shut our eyes to them and pretend they are not there. All we plead for is that they be seen against the background of the Passion of Christ. Evil and suffering are a large question mark in the world of today, and a question mark they will remain to the end. A partial answer might be gleaned from what we have just been saying, like this: The sorrows and the trials of this life, our own and those of others, offer a magnificent opportunity of rising to great heights of divine love. It is a simple enough matter to practice our faith and consider ourselves to be good Catholics as long as we are sailing along happily in a calm sea with a pleasant sun shining over our heads and a gentle breeze behind. The real testing to our faith comes when storms toss the boat up and down, when wind and rain blind our eyes, when we have to bare our arms, seize both oars and row for all we are worth against a strong current.

As for the sufferings of our neighbor, to see Christ's Passion being reproduced in them, to relieve and console others from that motive — this is a sure way of laying the axe to those roots of selfishness that warp the spiritual life of so many of us.

"There is no answer to the problem of evil," writes Father John McKenzie, "and no way to meet the evil in the concrete, except suffering and death. We have seen men in all ages try to shake off the burden by the most various and ingenious devices, and they have all failed. Jesus alone came and said: 'Take up your cross; if you wish to find joy, suffer.' He did not explain it. He simply lived that way. If there were a better answer to the problem, it is hard to think that the incarnate God would not have chosen it."

The influence of a person who succeeds in learning this very difficult lesson and living by it — a worldwide influence in the souls of men — is beautifully described in a passage packed with material for meditation and prayer. It occurs in a book by a Poor Clare Colettine called *Songs in the Night*, and this is how it goes:

"What each soul is interiorly," she writes, "face to face with God, unknown to anyone, is of vital consequence to all the human race, and every act of love toward God, every act of faith and adoration, every mute uplifting of the heart, raises the whole Church, yea the whole world, nearer to God.

"From each soul that is in union with God and at rest in the divine embrace, there radiates a spiritual vitality, a light and strength and joy, which reaches from end to end of the universe, a source of grace even to those least worthy of it, even to those least conscious of it, and knowing nothing of whence or how it came. All humanity is drawn into the soul's encounter with the divine lover, and thrills to their mutual love. All creation is moved by the secret word spoken by God within the soul. All creation shares in the soul's silent, hidden communion with God.

"Lord, Jesus Christ, I entreat thee to let me find in thy presence a strong defense, protection and safeguard. Let thy wounds be my food and drink, to nourish and make me drunk with delight. Let the shedding of thy blood wash all my offenses away; let thy death bring me the life that knows no ending; may thy cross be my everlasting glory. In these may my heart find renewal and gladness and health and delight. So I hope. So may it be!"

As we close this introductory chapter we feel a firm confidence that it may have deepened our conviction that the Passion is relevant in our day; that it may have started up a hunger and a craving to taste its sweetness with new delight, and that the pages now to follow may whet the reader's appetite for more. More there always will be. Take from infinity as much as ever you wish, and infinity still remains.

St. John, who never tires of speaking about love, wants to hold us up for a minute before allowing us to pass on to the next chapter. He wrote this sentence: "God so loved the world that he gave his only-begotten son" (John 3:16). He is anxious to make sure we do not miss the deep significance of that little word "so." We estimate a person's appreciation of an object by the price he is willing to pay for it. A piece of land, a rare book or picture or manuscript, a latest-model car — if objects such as these come on the market and are to be sold by public auction they will go to the highest bidder. The more keen is the prospective buyer on getting what he has set his heart upon, the more determined will he be to outbid everyone else.

· So vast is God's love for us that He gave nothing less to us than His own Son with the gifts He brought to us. That Son, in His turn, offers us a proof of love greater than which no man has, that he lays down his life for his friends. "God *so* loved . . ." — with the utmost reverence we say it — that He is the highest bidder. No one will He permit to outbid Him.

The mystery deepens when we ask ourselves why God so loves us — why He loves *me*. I am a creature of His hand, absolutely dependent on Him for every breath I draw. I am one of the millions of men who have lived since creation began, one of the millions alive today and of the millions still to come. What an infinitesimal drop am I in the ocean of humanity! What does God find that makes Him so love me and crave my love in return? I remember the prayer of St. Francis, repeated all through the night as he knelt on Mount Alverno: "Lord, who are You and what am I?" The immense gap between the "allness" of God and the nothingness of the creature!

Why does He love, and "so" love? We have to confess that the answer eludes us. The mystery remains, but the fact is beyond dispute.

THE CAST

MARY, MOTHER OF GOD

There is one command, only one, which has been put on record as having issued from Our Lady. It is very comprehensive. In some ways it might be regarded as a summary of the entire gospel teaching. It alone has formed the saints, supplying them with a sure test in arriving at right decisions, whatever the circumstances. It provides a motive and incentive to overcome difficulties. Mary had found it as she meditatively turned the pages of the Old Testament. She saw it acted out in its full perfection as she lived close to Jesus and observed how He advanced in wisdom, age, and grace before God and man.

She had been invited to come with Him and His apostles to a marriage celebration. It is very probable that she made herself useful in preparing the meal and seeing to the needs of the guests as each one took his place at the table. Long before this event she had described herself as "the handmaid of the Lord" — a person who always held herself in readiness to obey His slightest wish. This role she fulfilled also at Cana. She moved about quietly, keeping a watchful eye to make sure that all arrangements were moving smoothly. She was the first to notice the possibility of a hitch, which, if not forestalled, would be an embarrassment to the young couple. The wine was running short, possibly because the apostles, though made welcome, arrived unexpectedly.

Mary tells Jesus, and Jesus orders the servants to fill six large waterpots with water. They did so, and to the astonishment of all, the water, when poured out, proved to be wine, far superior in quality to any the guests had tasted since the beginning of the celebrations.

And Mary's command? The only command known ever to fall from her lips? She told the waiters: "Whatever he [her Son] tells you to do, do it." That this sentence expresses her own habitual frame of mind is evident from her "fiat": "Be it done to me according to your word" (Luke 1:38). She thus placed herself unreservedly in the hands of God, prepared to give unquestioning obedience to His will in all things. Her instructions to the waiters at Cana are the expression of the underlying principle which ruled Mary's every thought, word and act.

Such acceptance, she was soon to learn, would call for suffering. When Simeon took her baby in his arms he blessed God, and then, turning to her, he spoke this ominous prophecy: "A sword shall pierce your own soul" (Luke 2:35).

Good Friday

It was especially in the Passion that she learned, experimentally, the truth of the words spoken by Simeon. On Good Friday Christ took on His shoulders His own cross and set out for Calvary and His crucifixion. Utterly exhausted, He fell several times. As He drags Himself to His feet after one of these falls and forces His eyes open, weighed down as they are with blood and spittle, He finds himself looking straight into the eyes of Mary, His mother. One thinks she must have had difficulty in even recognizing Him. From her place here at the corner of the street she stands and looks and stares, incredulous. What have they done to Him? "Despised, and the most abject of men, a man of sorrows and acquainted with infirmity." "Whatever he shall say to you . . ." There are two details in this scene that seem difficult to understand at first sight. It might occur to us, first, to suggest that if Christ really loved His mother it is surprising that He did not spare her this bitter sorrow. It could so easily have been arranged. Why, for instance, did He not so plan things that His mother would be up at Nazareth during these days and that she would know nothing of His Passion till it was all over and had given place to the joys of the Resurrection?

We rightly admire people who try to hide their pains or make light of them to spare their friends from sharing them. At this very moment as I sit here typing a young Carmelite brother is suffering intensely from cancer of the throat. He will certainly have gone to God long before this book is published. He has been in this condition for two years. To swallow even a drop of water is torture; to speak a few words calls for a mighty effort. But never is there a complaint, never an impatient gesture; for everyone who visits him he has a beautiful smile of welcome. Everyone loves him. Nothing does he leave undone to hide his sufferings and spare his parents and friends any grief he can possible prevent.

But here on the way to Calvary Jesus has deliberately so arranged things that His mother is with Him, seeing Him in this shocking state, listening to the coarse jeers of His executioners, who spit in His face, kick Him when He stumbles, forcing Him to His feet each time and goading Him forward when He is scarcely able to stand. Each fall is a stab of pain to the mother's heart. All the motherly instinct in her rose up and urged her to step forward and do something, anything, to bring Him some measure of relief. But she can do nothing except stand there aghast, powerless, unable even to lift her arms and give Him some support.

Naim

Until we reflect it seems astounding and incredible that such a son could have let such a mother in for such agony when He need not have done so. We wonder the more when we recall Christ's attitude toward another brokenhearted mother, the widow of Naim. He met her as she was walking after the coffin of her only son on the way to the grave. She was weeping, and He told her in soothing tones to dry her eyes. He was obviously filled with compassion. He halted the cortege, laid His hand on the bier and ordered the dead man to arise. "And the dead man sat up and began to talk, and Jesus gave him to his mother."

What joy and stupefaction this miracle brought to the mother's heart we are left to surmise. Jesus, His gracious deed done, seems to have moved on out of the picture, while "everyone was filled with awe and praised God, saying: 'A great prophet has appeared among us; God has visited his people' " (Luke 7:11-17).

The contrast between Christ's treatment of Mary, His mother, and the widow of Naim surprises us. We may be tempted to ask if He really did love Mary. We may be inclined to think He must have loved the widow of Naim more. If so, we are wrong. "My thoughts are not your thoughts," He tells us. "My ways are not your ways — it is the Lord who speaks. Yes, the heavens are as high above the earth as my ways are above your ways, and my thoughts above your thoughts" (Isaiah 55. 8-9).

Coming back to our question, we ask: "Why so much compassion for the widow of Naim and so little, it would seem, for His mother?" The answer deserves our most serious, prolonged, and prayerful meditation. He took away the cross from the widow but brought it deliberately into the heart of His mother *because He loved Mary immeasurably more than He loved the widow of Naim*. It was in the divine plan that the love of Mary for God was to transcend all the love for Him given to Him by the rest of creation. Christ's love of the Father, was of course, unique and supreme, but once that has been clearly stated, we can go on to say that after Christ's love the love of God's mother for God is like the blazing sunshine at noon and the love of the rest of creation is like the moon and stars. Mary, the great lover, is "a woman clothed with the sun, and the moon under her feet" (Revelation 12:1).

What is the most searching test of love? Undoubtedly it is the willing acceptance of suffering and the cross. This is the proof *par excellence*. This purifies the heart by detaching it from what is of earth and attaching it to the things of heaven. In Our Lady's case there was no need for purification as she was sinless from the first moment of her conception. All her sufferings, therefore, were employed exclusively to attach her each day more closely to God. She grew in grace, in union with Him, because she abandoned herself unreservedly to Him. She lived out her "fiat," and this entailed that after Christ no one would suffer more. Because God willed her sanctity to attain to such high eminence, therefore He provided her with abundant material from which to weave the garment of holiness.

To qualify for the position destined for her, unique among all the lovers of God, Our Lady had to undergo a gruelling test. She was to participate more fully in the Passion of her divine Son than any other individual person, than all others combined. "O all ye who pass by this way, attend and see if there be any sorrow like my sorrow" (Lamentations 1:12). God willed her to share close in the Passion, so Christ took good care that His mother should be present throughout. He could not afford to allow her miss such a marvelous opportunity of growing in love. The sword must pass through her heart even though it pierced Him too.

If we but realize it, to hold up the streams of grace by sin or deliberate imperfection even in a lesser degree, to let slip through our fingers one single opportunity of growing in divine love through sanctified suffering, is a greater disaster than all the temporal evils of today and from the beginning of the world.

A Mother's Prayer

There is another question we would like to raise concerning Mary and the Passion. Jesus loved His mother, but we saw His love expressing itself in a way we would not have expected at first sight. We now turn to Mary's love for Him and find what seems to be another anomaly in the way she manifests it. Would it not seem reasonable to suggest that she might have taken some steps to have the case of her Son dismissed or at least to have the terrible sentence mitigated? Should she not make the attempt? Pilate, the judge, was after all not without some humanity in his character. He had not completely silenced the voice of conscience. He was weak and hesitant and wavering. He was tortured by doubts and scruples and superstitions. Just now he was tense and nervous as a result of the urgent message brought to him from Claudia Procula, his wife: "Have nothing to do with that just man, for I have suffered many things in a dream because of him" (Matthew 27:19).

Suppose Mary had approached this vacillating judge at an early stage of the trial, when Pilate was first confronted by the Jews and their prisoner. Suppose she had fallen down on her knees before him, weeping and explaining that Jesus was her only child, and that the evidence was overwhelming that "He has done all things well" (Mark 7:37). Suppose she had appealed to his conscience and reminded him that he must render to God a strict account of the manner in which he administered the authority committed to him. Suppose she insisted that this particular trial was different from any other in which he had had to adjudicate before, carrying as it did a really terrifying responsibility. Suppose she had enlisted the cooperation of Claudia to strengthen her case. Would her prayer have prevailed? Would it have been possible for a poor unknown country woman to make her way through the crowds and gain access to Pilate and win his attention and sympathy? Our supposition would seem to have validity even in spite of the serious difficulties these questions raise. Would we agree that most mothers, if they found themselves in Our Lady's position, would seize on the opportunity to make these representations if offered, prepared to take a chance? They would argue that they had nothing to lose and something might be gained. Pilate, at all times easy to sway, might be more likely to listen and yield in his present state of indecision and agitation.

We know, of course, that not a syllable of that prayer ever fell from the lips of Mary. Mary said nothing. Mary did nothing to save or protect her Son or secure some mitigation for Him. But the whole point of this supposition is that *even if she was certain* she would succeed in influencing Pilate in this way, she would have refrained from making any interference. She would have reacted exactly as we know her actually to have done. Not a word of petition or protest; not a plea for mercy to judges or soldiers or the mob. She stood and watched it all. She followed Him step by step. We have no record of anything she may have said. Presently we shall suggest that she probably did not even weep. Because all this was the practical working out of her "fiat," God permitted His Son to suffer like this. All she had to do was say "Amen," and she said it from her heart. Does this not show that we have got things all wrong when we think or say that God is cruel, that He allows suffering to fall upon us because He wants to punish us?

"Begone, Satan!"

St. Matthew, in his sixteenth chapter, throws further light on the true answer. Christ had just made Peter the rock on which to build His church. He had given him the keys of the kingdom of heaven, with the power to bind and to loosen. But before Peter has had time to reflect on the privileges thus heaped upon him, he hears himself severely reprimanded by the Christ who had just exalted him. "Get behind me, Satan! You are a scandal to me. The way you think is not God's way but man's" (Matt. 16:23). Satan — the name recalls the stern command given to the devil when he tempted Christ in the desert: "Begone, Satan!"

Peter is Satan too! Why? Christ has just been telling His disciples about the Passion He would soon have to face, culminating in His death on the cross. Poor Peter, ardent lover of his master, is horrified. He draws Our Lord aside and begins to remonstrate. This evil must be averted. Peter will see to it. A counterattack must be launched to foil the plans of those who would dare to touch Christ with evil intent. The Master need have no fear. Let Him leave the situation in Peter's hands and all will be well. Peter, of course, had the very best of intentions. He loved Christ with a deep, tender affection, but as yet it was mostly a natural love, such as he might have had for any good man. Christ chided him. All unwittingly, Peter was making himself a tool in the hands of Satan by his opposition to the cross.

A young man in his early twenties was walking up the garden path leading to the home of his parents. He stopped short, reeled and fell. Father and mother rushed out and carried him in. He lived for less than an hour. They were brokenhearted, especially as he was an only son. Weeks later they were still talking about the calamity. Said the mother: "Why is God so hard on us? We are trying sincerely to lead good Catholic lives, and see what he has done to us!" A very human cry, deserving of our deep sympathy. But was that excellent mother right? I feel sure she believed she was. Peter thought he was right too.

Calvary marks the climax to the "fiat" of Our Lady. Poets and artists sometimes represent her at the cross, swooning in excessive grief into the arms of John, or throwing up her hands in a dramatic gesture, meant to indicate the greatness of her sorrow. Such productions have a worthy object. They are intended to be graphic representations of what actually happened. But it must be confessed that they do little to honor Mary or foster solid piety, being nothing more than the product of the fertile imagination of the artist or poet.

What we know on the authority of the gospel is that "there stood by the cross of Jesus his mother..." (John 19:25). She stood there, seemingly for nearly three hours unbroken, watching, waiting, praying, accepting it all, loving the sword piercing her very soul. Did she even weep? Probably not. Tears would have given an outlet, a relief. But they would not come. "There are tears which at their fountains freeze."

A mother was officially informed that her son, with several others, had been killed. The body was lying on a bed in hospital, and she was asked to go and identify it. She described to me what happened. She was shown into a large ward with fifteen beds on each side, on nearly every bed a corpse. My friend looked at the first, and the second, and the third — no, none of these was her son. She moved on to six and seven — yes, there he was, and she pointed to the last bed, in the corner. There were no tears, no hysterics. She stood there, mute and apparently not caring. But as on Calvary, her grief was too deep for any external manifestation. She was dulled and atrophied, standing and staring, just barely able to endure her sorrow. "There are tears which at their fountains freeze."

On Good Friday our redemption was accomplished. Did Mary, too, stand in need of redemption? Yes, for she is a creature of God, even though her role in history is unique, even though she be, as the Protestant poet calls her so fittingly and so beautifully, "our tainted nature's solitary boast."

So she too was redeemed, but in a manner far surpassing ours, and this is much to say when we remember what we read about the work of our redemption on another page. What was the difference?

We were redeemed by the merits of Christ, which were applied to us *after* the death on Calvary. But in the case of Our Lady these merits were applied *in advance* of the Passion. These were foreseen, and because they were certain to follow on His death, Mary was given the benefit of them beforehand. Thus she was conceived and born immaculate as befitted the woman who was to be mother of God.

Pope Pius XII

For Mary, as for Jesus, Calvary is the beginning, not the end. For it has culminated for Christ in the Resurrection and Ascension, and for Mary in her Assumption. Because Christ is God we speak of His *Ascension*, which implies that He went back to heaven by His own divine power. Nobody did it for Him. Nobody cooperated with Him. He went back, just as He had come down, because He willed it. But Mary was *assumed* into heaven. She was taken up by God, on whom she depended completely to do this thing for her.

In November, 1950, Pope Pius XII solemnly defined as a revealed dogma of the Catholic faith that Mary was taken up, body and soul, into heaven on coming to the end of her life here on earth. He states: "After We had many times offered prayers of supplication to God and invoked the light of the spirit of truth, for the glory of almighty God who gave a special love to the Virgin Mary ... in order to increase the glory of this august mother and to give joy and exaltation to the whole church. ... We pronounce, declare and define, by the authority of Our Lord Jesus Christ, and that of the apostles Peter and Paul, and Our Own, that it is a divinely-revealed dogma that Mary, immaculate mother and ever a virgin, having ended her sojourn of life here on earth, was assumed, body and soul, into the glory of heaven."

This, the Pope said afterwards, was "the supreme moment of Our pontificate." Catholics adhere to their devotion to Mary because it is taught them by the Church. "It proceeds from true faith," says Vatican II, "by which we are led to know the excellence of the mother of God, and are moved to a filial love towards our mother and to the imitation of her virtues" (*Lumen Gentium* 67). It is no argument at all against any dogma of the Church — as was said when the assumption was defined — that there is no evidence for it in Scripture. We learn what Christ taught not only from the Bible, but also from the living voice of the living Church, founded by Him to teach it to us, and enriched with a promise from Him that He will preserve His Church from error when she is so teaching.

What, then, do I believe about Mary? Here is an attempt at the answer, which must always remain inadequate: I believe that, from the first instant of her conception Mary was free from the stain of the sin we all inherit, and that right through her whole life she never sinned. I believe that her soul was full of grace from the first instant it left the Creator's hands and that with the years she grew continually in this divine life. I believe that Mary is in the most literal sense mother of Jesus Christ, who is true God and true man, one in nature with the Father and Holy Spirit, and equal to them in all things.

I believe that she is mother in an altogether miraculous manner, unprecedented and never to be repeated, for I am certain that she conceived Jesus Christ without the cooperation of a human father, and that therefore she is virgin and mother. I know that she is mother of all persons who constitute the mystical body of her Son, since they form with Him one great organism, they being the branches and He the vine. I know that at the moment she left this world she was taken up body and soul into heaven, and "exalted by the Lord as queen of all, in order that she might be the more thoroughly conformed to her Son, the Lord of lords and the conqueror of sin and death."

Mary has shown herself repeatedly in our day and spoken words of the gravest warning concerning the prevalence of sin, and she insists that if a global war is to be averted we Catholic Christians must take seriously to heart the need to give ourselves to prayer and season our prayer with penance.

JOHN

Have you ever had the experience of reaching the final stage of your train journey and expecting to see your best friend waiting for you on the platform? You jump up from your seat, fling the door open and look out eagerly. Hundreds, perhaps thousands, are crowded there before you, but your glance passes swiftly from one to another. You are interested in only *the* one. On catching sight of him you leap down from your carriage and elbow your way in his direction. No one else matters. The presence of all the others would count for nothing if he was absent.

Is it possible that Jesus Christ could be all this to us? That the heart within us would burn at the very mention of His name? When the lover is Jesus and the person loved begins to learn experimentally the utter truth and sincerity and beauty of what Christ has to give, he finds himself speechless in face of this new and awesome reality. The more human love is an overflowing of the divine love, the more surely will it fill the vacuum in our hearts. But human love, no matter how pure and perfect, could never compete with the love of the God-man. It expresses itself in a universal love for all men. It is not exclusive, like the love I have for my friend on the platform, for in every human being it recognizes Jesus Himself. The image may be sadly distorted and disguised, but the true lover who has "learned Christ" will know how to pierce through that disguise and discover Him behind it.

The craving to persuade us of this truth, a craving born of personal experience, vibrates in everything written for us by the evangelist St. John. He holds a prominent position in the school of love. He is dedicated to his task. He indicates the course he intends to follow on the very first day we enter his classroom. He foresees that he is going to be preoccupied with Christ as the lectures proceed. "Something that existed from the beginning," he explains, "something that we have heard and have seen with our eyes, that we have watched and have touched with our hands — the Word who is life — This is our subject."

We must not miss the gradation here, the steady progress from one degree of knowledge of Christ to another. John's first experience was to *hear* about Christ from others. His interest is aroused. So he makes it his business to *see* Him — just a passing glance, perhaps, such as you might give to an object displayed in a shop window or to the title of a chapter in a book. But John went much farther. He has *watched* Christ, and we know what a difference there is between seeing and watching. John has not merely taken notice of the object in the shop window; he has gone into the store to examine it more carefully. He has not just looked casually at the chapter heading; he has brought the book home, making a profound study of the entire volume, chapter by chapter, till he has become a recognized authority on all it contains. This is what is meant when he tells us he watched Christ, studying His way of life, absorbed by the principles underlying it and inspired with its ideals. Finally comes the climax, when John *touches* Christ with his hands, verifying for himself that Jesus is real.

This is the schedule John proposes to every student entering his school. The whole course is summarized in three words: "God is love."

The two terms "God" and "love" are interchangeable. Our efforts to define God are doomed to failure. John here goes as far as it is possible for us to go when he tells us that "God" and "love" are synonymous.

And "God so loved the world as to give his only-begotten Son." Hence in his next session our teacher goes on to state that "if God has so loved us, then we ought also to love one another." He never wearies of inculcating this truth. Even in his extreme old age, when he had moved past a century, the theme on his lips was always the same. Before he died at Ephesus, he would have himself carried in to preside at the meetings of the brethren. What did he have to say to them? "My little children, love one another." After a while some in the audience felt slightly bored by the constant repetition and suggested that he give them something else. No change was necessary, the old man assured them, for "love is the fulfilling of the law."

Father William Doyle

There is a clear echo of John's teaching in the impassioned spiritual diary of an Irish Jesuit, the late Father William Doyle. Here is a typical excerpt: "Jesus is the most loving of lovable friends. There never was a friend like Him before, and there never will be one equal to Him, because there is only one Jesus in the whole wide world and the vast expanse of heaven; and that most sweet and loving friend, that true lover of the holiest and purest love, is *my* Jesus, mine alone and all mine. Every fibre of His divine nature is throbbing with love for me; every beat of His gentle heart is a throb of affection for me; His sacred arms are around me; He draws me to His breast. ... In the eyes of the vast world, the myriads of other souls all have vanished. He has forgotten them all; for that brief moment they do not exist, for even the infinite love of God Himself is not enough to pour out on the soul who is clinging to Him so lovingly. . . ."

Father Doyle's biographer, the late Msgr. O'Rahilly, comments as follows on this passage: "Doubtless there are stolid souls who will not appreciate these emotional outpourings, who regard such fervent language as mere sentimentalism. It is true, of course, that these utterances were never meant to be dragged from their sacred privacy into the cold light of print. But that is just the beauty of them. They well up spontaneously from the heart of a strong man. They express the pent-up enthusiasm of this brave soldier of Christ, seeking an unconventional outlet. Father Doyle was no sickly sentimentalist or hysterical weakling. He lived what he felt and he meant what he said. Why should we fancy that strength should be shorn of tenderness? Why should we think that only earthly love is privileged to have its delights?"

Why, indeed? — except that we are not convinced and, as John will show us presently, because our thinking has gone awry.

"What is more grotesque," asks Msgr. Benson, "in the eyes of the unimaginative world, than the ecstasy of the lover? Common sense never yet drove a man mad. It is common sense which is thought to characterize sanctity, and therefore common sense has never scaled mountains, much less has it cast them into the sea. But it is the maddening joy of the conscious companionship of Jesus Christ which has produced the lovers, and therefore the giants of history. It is the developing friendship of Jesus Christ, *and of his passion*, which has inspired these lives which the world in its dull moments calls unnatural and the Church in all her moods calls supernatural."

Lostness

All this leads us to repeat what we have said already — that the world's most pressing need is to bring Christ back; to renew within us an appreciation of the fact that we are loved, personally and collectively, by Christ and that He has gone to Calvary to prove the truth of that love. For we have to make the sad admission that we have lost Christ, entirely or in large measure. Apart from the two hundred millions who, says Vatican II, have not even heard His name, there are those of us who call ourselves Catholics and Christians and yet hate and calumniate and plunder and murder one another. Further, we could draw a picture of Catholics who are lukewarm, who serve God as if He were a Shylock, reluctantly putting in an appearance at Mass, receiving the sacraments rarely and without relish and muttering a few incoherent prayers, just because they are afraid this tyrannical God might send them to hell! What do they know or care about John's sublime teaching on divine love?

Christ was lost even by His parents, through no fault of their own, in the crowds thronging the streets of Jerusalem. One cannot but feel an acute anxiety lest, in the religious discussions and seminars and courses that abound, Christ should be crushed out. Do all those views elaborated on in the new theology develop in us that deep personal love of Christ so insistently urged upon us in the school of St. John? Do they deepen our faith in the Real Presence of Christ in the Eucharist or sow doubts about it in our minds? Is the Mass more meaningful to us as being the same identical sacrifice as Calvary, because of the deplorable lack of reverence with which it is at times celebrated? Are we in danger of losing that filial love of Mary that has always been the hallmark of a genuinely Catholic life? There is a lack of unction, a want of warmth in our religion as it is often presented to us in these days.

"I sincerely believe," wrote the late Cardinal John Heenan, "that, in addition to seeping physical energy, the present burden of talk produces a weariness of the spirit, leading to narcissism and the neglect of personal prayer. People who talk excessively rarely pause to listen to God in prayer."

We are very commonsense about all this, of course; we are objective in our approach to God, scared lest we betray that deep personal devotion to Christ that might be construed into "a maddening joy." "If you rely more on your own reason than upon the virtue that submits to Jesus Christ, you will seldom or hardly become an enlightened man. For God will have us wholly subject to Him and to transcend (not contradict) all reason by an inflamed love." So Thomas à Kempis believed and taught, but have we lost him too in the confusion caused all around us by a babel of voices?

Asceticism is a museum piece, a relic of bygone days. Instead we hear much about love for one another, about care and concern, and here we seem to be putting into practice what we learned in the school of St. John. The difficulty is that we so often seem to forget the supernatural motive, which he never fails to stress. So our "charity" degenerates into an artificial joviality, a boisterous hail-fellow-well-metness. This may, in fact, be nothing more than a transplant into our Christian community of the urbane, conventional tolerance and humanism that normally pervade a secular, pagan club. Pagans, after all, can be quite charming people.

Contacts

John and his brother James earned their living by fishing. Their father Zebedee had been in the business before them. At the time of Christ all three plied the trade, spending most of the day and often nearly the whole night casting their nets into the waters of Lake Gennesaret and hauling them out again. It seems likely that they heard some of their neighbors talking about John the Baptizer, about his strange way of life and the forthright manner in which he preached. They decided, with their father's approval, to take a few days off to visit him and find out who he was and what was his mission. There was a rumor that he might even be the long-expected Messiah.

Their first contact with Christ could have come about in this way. They found Him walking alone down along the bank of the Jordan. The Baptizer had pointed Him out to them, telling them He was the Lamb of God who takes away the sins of the world. The two brothers walked behind at a respectful distance, keeping Him in view. When the three of them were clear of the crowd Jesus turned His head, saw them, and asked them the most natural question in the world. "You seem to be looking for someone; who is it?" They were slightly embarrassed. The fact was, of course, that they were tracking Him down, but they were somewhat reluctant to say so. After an awkward moment or two they found their tongues and answered His question by blurting out another. "Master," they said, "where do you live?" "Come and see" was the immediate invitation. So "they came and saw the place where he lived, and they stayed with him all that day." It was John's first meeting with Christ, and we have no difficulty in believing that from the beginning of that interview both he and his brother James felt powerfully attracted to Him. We do not know what they talked about, but in another text we are told that "never did man speak like this man." Again, elsewhere, we read that the people He addressed sat listening with eyes fixed upon Him, marvelling at the sweetness and graciousness of the words falling from His lips. There was also that memorable evening of the first Easter Sunday when He joined His two disciples on the road to Emmaus and their hearts burned within them as they listened.

The two visitors had never had an experience like this in their whole lives. There was something about this man, Jesus of Nazareth, which made Him different from any other person they had ever met. They gladly yielded to the attraction they felt. There is significance in the statement that "they stayed with him all that day."

So obviously did He love them! Later John, with pardonable pride, would refer to himself more than once as "the disciple whom Jesus loved." Some weeks later, days perhaps, Jesus made a return call. He saw James, we read, son of Zebedee, and his brother John, sitting in a boat with their father, mending their nets. He called them "and at once, leaving their father and the boat, they followed him." They seemed to themselves to have no option. It was the most natural thing in the world for them to do. Where was He going? What did He want? How long were they to remain with Him? These questions do not seem to have even entered their minds. Nothing mattered except to be with Him. The nets fell out of their hands. They stepped from the boat onto the shore "at once." They never looked back.

On that day John was registered as a student in the school

of love. He was keen and quick to learn, and he made rapid progress. Under such a highly qualified teacher and given his own responsiveness, things could scarcely have been different. Constant contact with Jesus served to convince him that there never was a friend like Him before and there would never again be His equal. From now on John had only one task to do — to try to persuade the whole world of the unspeakable joy it is missing if it loses Jesus in the crowd.

Plaster Saint?

But please do not think of John as an anemic, spineless, sugary character, oozing piousness, afraid to assert himself, lacking moral courage. Not at all. For all his sweetness and gentleness, he could hit straight from the shoulder whenever the occasion demanded it. He had a shocking bad habit of telling a man he was a liar! If, for example, someone professes to love God and at the same time hates his brother the silver-tongued John has no hesitation in telling him: "You are a liar! If you do not love your brother whom you see, how can you possibly love God whom you do not see?" Again: "Anyone who says, 'I love God,' and does not keep his commandments is a liar and the truth is not in him." Jesus called John and James the sons of thunder. Perhaps this was because of the impatience they showed and expressed whenever they came upon smugness or hypocrisy or cant of any kind.

There is evidence of this same impetuosity and intolerance in an episode one evening in a Samaritan village. It was getting late, and not one person in the place was prepared to give Jesus a bed for the night. Samaritans and Jews were traditional enemies, so they told this wandering Jewish preacher from Nazareth to look somewhere else for lodgings. John, so sweet and loving and gentle, had a brilliant idea. "Lord," he said, "shall we call down fire from heaven upon them, wipe them out and burn their petty town to the ground?" A nice Christian wish that was! John was still a learner, still sitting in the elementary classroom of the school of love. The Master warned him on this occasion that he did not know the spirit of evil lurking in his suggestion.

The Twelve had a group discussion one day as they walked and talked together. The subject of the debate was as futile as some of those concerning which we had hard things to say a while ago. They were trying to decide which of them was the greatest man in the group! When Our Lord joined them later on He asked them pointedly what they had been talking about. There was an uncomfortable silence. They may have colored a little, being unwilling to answer; maybe they tried to divert the conversation into another channel. Jesus, with exquisite tact, found His own way of setting them right. Putting His arms around a little child who happened to be standing near, He told them: "The one who makes himself as little as this little child is the greatest in the kingdom of heaven."

They were ambitious too, covetous of notoriety, anxious to show off — John and his brother, perhaps, more so than the others. We say this because of a request made to Christ by Salome, mother of James and John. It seems reasonable enough to think that the three of them had hatched the plot together. What was it? Jesus, people were saying, had come to found a kingdom. Salome kept an eye on Christ. She had something to whisper in His ear. The chance came and she said to Him: "Lord, when you do found this new kingdom will you please allow my two boys to have the first places, one on your right hand and one on your left?" The other apostles, we read, were indignant with the two brothers for allowing this scheme to go through — perhaps because each of them had an eye on that privileged position for himself!

So John was no plaster saint. He had plenty of the very human traits we find in ourselves. As he continued to frequent more and more the company of his Master, he assimilated His mentality. He began to discover a somewhat childish folly and secret pride running through his whole life, unseen and un-suspected until now. "You know not of what spirit you are," Christ had warned him. Under the action of grace in his soul he would gradually be cleansed of even these lesser faults and prove himself all the more worthy to be the disciple whom Jesus loved.

Tabor

We have an outstanding event in the story of John as he draws near the "finals" in Christ's school of love. This is the transfig-uration on Mount Tabor. Christ usually drew His apostles "apart" whenever He had a special message to give them or some important lesson to teach them. Thus He called them "apart" into the desert to pray and to meditate. When they failed to grasp some point in His public utterances He would draw them "apart" later on and explain it to them. Tabor, too, is a place "apart." It has been compared to a massive high altar raised up by God for the glorification of His Son. It rises, awe-inspiring in its sheer majesty, till it reaches the height of nearly two thousand feet above the level of the Mediterranean.

To this eminence Jesus conducted Peter, James, and John when He had planned to favor them with a special revelation.

"He led them into a high mountain *apart* and was transfig-ured before them. His face shone like the sun and his garments became white as snow." It would seem as if, for one fleeting in-stand, He allowed the rays of His divinity to penetrate through the veil of His humanity. The three men were alarmed but also intoxicated with joy.

Peter would like this to go on forever. He would be glad to forget all about the drab valleys below and the trivialities by which men are preoccupied, now so clearly seen to be of little importance in the light of this vision. The others felt the same, but Christ's purpose in granting them this favor was quite dif-ferent.

Contemplative prayer such as this, in which Christ is in some manner transfigured before us, is admirably described in *Songs in the Night* by a Poor Clare Colettine. "Who can express how sweet, how solemn, how subtle, how penetrating is this interior song of the life of love? As the soul listens it knows that it is being taught wonderful things, for it is drawn close to the mysteries of God and lives under their influence. It is the 'disciplina arcani' — the awe and reverence imposed by the hidden and incomprehensible things of God."

But this experience will not last. Prayer ordinarily alternates between consolation and desolation. In desolation there is "a famine for God. The soul tastes to the full what real loneliness is, for God is gone. The silence is sterile. The former generous ardor has grown as cold as dead ashes. . . ."

In John's case Tabor was a forerunner and a preparation for the terrible darkness and desolation of Gethsemani and Calvary. The last supper was the immediate prelude. "The disciple whom Jesus loved" occupied a privileged position that night, seated next to Christ and leaning his head against His breast. Thence he drew the ineffable secrets of the Sacred Heart and gave them to us in sublime language.

It must have cost him a big effort to pass over in silence any reference to the Blessed Eucharist. The very probable explanation is that the other three evangelists had already described it in detail, and throughout his gospel John is mainly concerned to set down events not previously put on record.

In the other three accounts we see Christ saying the first Mass, ordaining His first priests and giving them their First Holy Communion. John passes all this by. But he has compensated us marvelously. He has won our undying gratitude by devoting no less than four full chapters to Our Lord's discourse after the meal. We shall try to say more about them on another page. For the moment they interest us insofar as they point to the sweet consolations Christ gave to John to prepare him for the darkness that would envelop his soul in the agony and at the crucifixion.

This power to sustain him John would need more than the others, for he alone, of all the Twelve, was the only one who stood by the cross of Jesus with Mary His mother.

John is represented by the eagle poised high up above our heads. He tells us that "God is light and in him there is no darkness." Like the eagle he soars, breaking through the dark clouds and plunging into that "light inaccessible" wherein dwells divinity. What he sees and describes might make us inclined to think he must have been favored with the splendor of the face-to-face "beatific vision" even while here on earth. We would be wrong, of course, for what he saw was no more than a dim ray from that shoreless ocean of light that is God.

We cannot refrain from quoting again from *Songs in the Night*. "God, God, God, in such a cry the soul pours itself forth in a sort of death, casting itself forth from self, into the desire of its heart — stripped of all thought that is not of Him — and, in a sort of birth, plunged into the very source of life, the beginning, wonderful, virginal, eternal. And when at last in the plenitude of joy the hymn subsides into silence and the soul folds its wings to drop, it is not back to self that it descends, but it falls to rest in His repose, as if it had soared so high that heaven was nearer than earth." In this light John is marvelously illuminated to see more deeply into the truth of the faith, to grasp with a new intelligence the meaning of the divine attributes. Realization replaces mere intellectual assent. He lifts us up with him and plunges us into this divine light in the very first chapter of his gospel. He is enthralled by the insight granted to him of the intimate life of God who "is" from the beginning. In time this universe leaped forth from His creative hands. "Through him all things came to be; not one thing but had its being through him." And God became a man like one of ourselves, except that in Him there was no sin. He came to make us, in the most literal sense, sons and daughters of God, who would actually have a real sharing in His own very life.

All this, and very much more, John saw, when, eagle-like,

he peered into the dazzling light falling down upon him from the face of God. After this illumination for his mind there follows, inevitably, in his contemplation, a warming for his heart. The things of earth grew strangely dim, though he will immerse himself in them to tell the world what he has seen and heard.

Clean of Heart

His contemplation, begun on Tabor, thus leads him into the light of a new knowledge of God and divine things, which is accompanied by a fire of divine love so vehement as to be contained only with difficulty in his heart. Finally, this experience of God cleanses the soul — "our God is a consuming fire" (Hebrews 12:29). This divine fire, so to say, penetrates into the very texture and innermost substance of the soul, drawing out of it its sins and imperfections in much the same way as the sun draws moisture from the earth. Just as fire changes everything into its own substance, so does divine grace shrivel up and destroy whatever would hinder God's complete possession of the soul.

"Blessed are the clean of heart for they shall see God."

The life of grace here on earth will be perfected and stabilized in heaven. Here, too, John is by our side to open our eyes and stir our hearts. Toward the end of his long life he was sent into exile on the island of Patmos. In this place where he was favored with a glimpse of heaven, which he finds, not surprisingly, difficult to describe in words. "My name is John," he tells us, "and through our union with Jesus I am your brother. . . . I was on the island of Patmos for having preached God's word . . . (Revelation 1:9).

"I saw a door open in heaven and heard the same voice speaking to me like a trumpet saying: 'Come up here: I will show you what is to come in the future.' With that the Spirit possessed me and I saw . . . a new heaven and a new earth . . . I heard a loud voice call from the throne: 'You see this city? Here

God lives among men. He will make his home with them: they shall be his people and he shall be their God ... He will wipe away all tears from their eyes and there will be no more death; nor mourning, nor sadness shall be any more, for the former things are passed away...' " (4:1-2; 21:1, 3, 4). We do not aspire to reach the heights scaled by St. John. But we can and we should accompany him a long way on the road to divine contemplation.

In his very valuable book *Christian Prayer*, Father Moschner writes: "Must we assume that only a few are predestined to receive these special gifts? Certainly not. More and more has the view been accepted that the mystical life of grace, which reaches its apex in contemplation, rightly belongs to every child of grace, to everyone reborn in Jesus Christ, because it is, in reality, nothing more than the perfection of the three theological virtues ... God Himself deepens and strengthens and kindles them in us.

"The soul can dispose itself for this with the help of God's grace and create favorable dispositions. But the increase itself, the growth in strength and maturity, is never the work of the soul's efforts. ... God alone infuses the theological virtues, and the more powerfully these three — faith, hope, and love — are activated in the soul by God, the more closely do we approach to the state of contemplation; always, however, this presupposes that the soul has been faithfully submissive to the gently-guiding direction of the Holy Spirit. It is this fidelity, we repeat, which constitutes our contribution, and God demands it."

"Earth's crammed with heaven
And every common bush alive with God.
And only he who sees takes off his shoes.
The rest sit around it and pick blackberries"
        (Elizabeth Barrett Browning).

MAGDALENE

In this section of our book we are sketching the background of the different characters who appear on the stage in the course of the drama. Before we begin to talk about Mary Magdalene we would like to refer to St. John's fourth chapter. There he shows us "Jesus, weary from his journey," seated at the well of Jacob. A Samaritan woman comes along. The afternoon is hot. Jesus is thirsty and tired, and He asks her for a drink of water. She stares at Him in astonishment. This is "not done." Jews and Samaritans ignored each other's existence. Jesus breaks the tradition. He explains to her the meaning of grace, using the water of the well to clarify His meaning. She is impressed, though she could not be expected to understand the full implication of His words.

Then comes a sudden digression. "Go," He says, "and call your husband. . . ." This puts her on the defensive at once. "I have no husband," she tells Him. "You are right to say, 'I have no husband,'" he answers, "for although you have had five, the one you have now is not your husband." He moves along quietly from there; by the time the interview is over the sinful woman has been transformed into an apostle. She rushes back into the city with the good news that she believes she has found the Messiah.

There is a special reason for recalling this story. It is to be noted that the woman comes to draw water alone and in the middle of the day. Both details are significant. The practice of the women was to wait till the cool of evening, when they all moved out together, chatting as they walked, and waiting for one another till the pitchers were filled. They then hoisted them onto their heads and returned, procession-like, as they had come. But would they tolerate in their company the poor woman who encountered Christ? Certainly not. They were the respectable, righteous, smug, self-satisfied religious folk, and she was a woman of the street. But Christ showed interest and concern and love, and she responded instantly. He might have excused Himself from bothering on the grounds that He was hot and thirsty and footsore and weary. But He knew that what she needed — what she was blindly searching for — was in His power to give, and this wiped out every other consideration.

He hits at this same self-complacency and contempt for others in the parable of the pharisee and the publican. The pharisee presented the Lord with a carefully-drawn-up catalogue of all his good deeds — fasting, praying, almsgiving. He has nothing to ask from God; a paragon of all the virtues and he knows it.

The publican crept into the temple, diffident, *gauche*, wanting to avoid calling attention to himself while he gave himself to God in prayer. He stood in the shadow just inside the door, not presuming to advance further. He bowed head and shoulders down low. He kept striking his breast with his hand and begging for the mercy of God. Again and again prayer rose up from the depths of his soul and formed itself on his lips. "God," he kept repeating, "be merciful to me, a sinner." The pharisee prayed: "I thank you, Lord, that I am not like *him*." If he but knew, it would have better fitted him had he said: "Lord, I thank you that *he* is not like *me*!"

Christ sat down to table to eat His dinner in the company of publicans and sinners. He was their friend, His enemies charged — insinuating, I suppose, that He was a sinner Himself. But in Him there was no sin, and that is why we never find Him speaking of Himself as a sinner, or asking His Father for forgiveness. "He was like us in all things, sin alone excepted." But to be called the friend of sinners was quite another matter. He did not deny it. Indeed He gloried in it. It drew from Him two parables, which, to this day, inspire hope and bring love back into the lives of those whom sin had led astray. St. Luke has them in his fifteenth chapter — "The Lost Sheep" and "The Prodigal Son." This latter is now known as "The Forgiving Father."

The Sinful Woman

All this is meant to lead up to the first recorded meeting between Jesus and Magdalene. Magdala, where she was staying, was a fashionable seaside resort, roughly halfway between Capharnaum and Tiberias. She was was a beautiful girl and she lived in opulence by selling her charms at whatever fancy price she named. This caused no comment. The people, by and large, were broad-minded and tolerant: human nature is human nature, and men and women should be allowed to live their own lives; what they did with life or left undone was nobody's business. At Magdala they had all the plausible answers we have inherited.

Simon, a pharisee, lived in easy circumstances in the town. He heard the weird tales being circulated about Jesus, a carpenter from Nazareth. It might be interesting to have him in for a meal. Simon and his aristocratic friends could meet him and question him and decide for themselves. He would probably feel somewhat overawed in this grand company; he was only a workingman from the country after all. But they would be very tolerant. They would make allowances if he showed himself ignorant of the conventions observed in high society. They would try to forestall his mistakes and turn a blind eye if he failed to take a hint.

It does not seem an exciting dinner party. The conversation is dull. The visitor does not obtrude himself. He is clearly out of his depth. Simon is sizing him up and decides that he is a person lacking personality. What people found in this man to account for his popularity leaves Simon guessing. Looking around the table he sees that his friends are bored and disappointed. Simon decides to speed up the rest of the meal and dispatch Jesus back to associate with people of his own intelligence and social standing.

His reflections are interrupted. The door has been flung open. The guests turn and look. There, framed in the doorway, stands Mary of Magdala, the woman in the city who was a sinner. This is surely a surprise. What can a person with her reputation mean by daring to show herself in the house of this highly respectable citizen? They would know the answer almost before the question had had time to form itself in their minds.

From the spot where she is standing Mary scrutinizes the face of Simon and the faces of each one of his guests in turn. She shows only a momentary interest until her searching gaze falls on Jesus the carpenter. Him she wants. Him and no other. How she first came to hear about Him we do not know. Perhaps she was one in the crowd listening to Him when He spoke, and His words somehow had burnt themselves into her mind and set her heart beating fast. What evil construction would those grand persons in Simon's house put upon her action if now she singled out Jesus as the object of her special attention? She did not know. She did not care. She felt sure that Jesus would understand, and that was all that mattered.

Despising the scowls and indignant gestures, she passes them by, one after the other. In front of the couch where Jesus reclines she stops dead and kneels reverently before Him. All the pent-up emotion in her heart is suddenly released: she sobs and weeps as if it were going to break. Breaking it was indeed, with shame and sorrow for her sins and with love for this man whom she knew to be without sin.

Silence reigns. They are sitting motionless with eyes riveted upon her, fascinated. What is going to happen next? Her tears fall hot and fast upon His feet. She dries them with the beautiful black hair flowing over her shoulders. More. She produces a box of precious ointment, breaks the box and pours out the contents, to the very last drop, over those feet. And Christ sits and permits all this to go on. He does not kick her away as the self-righteous pharisees would do had she come to any one of them. Jesus lets her stay there, for just as long as she likes. We are told He drove seven devils out of her, perhaps meaning the seven capital sins — pride, covetousness, lust, anger, gluttony, envy and sloth. Perhaps that exorcism took place on that day, in this fashionable dining room, all unknown to the host and his guests, realized only by the poor girl herself and her merciful deliverer.

The onlookers are at first horrified and scandalized or affect to be. This amorous demonstration between the carpenter and the street girl, enacted here before them, is a monstrous insult to the owner of the house. Why does Simon not get up and throw the pair of them out into the street and slam his door and lock it? But after the first shock of asonishment their indignation cools down, giving place to a feeling of intense delight. For only now does it suddenly occur to them that Jesus is trapped. The secret is out. The woman has revealed it. They feel they cannot be mistaken. Everything points to the one conclusion.

Mercy

So the mighty prophet, eloquent in word and powerful in work, the preacher of such high morality, who knew so well how to denounce sin, is now exposed before the world for what he really is. Jesus the hypocrite, Jesus the liar, Jesus slave to a mistress, Jesus the blasphemer, Jesus the sorcerer, Jesus the exorcist who drove out devils by the power of Beelzebub, Jesus fair to behold externally but inwardly full of vice and corruption, Jesus whited sepulchre! Why, they could compose a whole litany to condemn him for his iniquities, snatching for the purpose even some of the phrases spoken by his own lips and now proved to express accurately the man's own appalling, intolerable double-facedness! To put that litany together and spread it far and wide would be a congenial task and they would lose no time in settling down to it.

Simon, too, was at first probably inclined to think along the same lines. But he soon rejected them. Jesus was no whited sepulcher. His whole life was transparently sincere. On another occasion he had challenged his accusers to convict him of sin and not one of them dared accept the challenge. So Jesus is not a sinner. But perhaps, thinks Simon, there is a chink in his armor just the same. Everyone in the area takes Magdalene for what she is. Surely if Jesus knew her real character he would have repulsed her. Apparently he does *not* know, and if this is so, he could not be the man sent from God, still less could he be the son of God whom he claimed to be. This Magdalene affair brings all his pretensions down around him like a house of cards.

Simon, so far, had given no external sign to suggest what was going on in his mind. He was naturally startled, then, when he heard Jesus addressing him directly and letting him see how clearly He read his thoughts. He told Simon about two debtors, one of whom owed fifty pence and the other five hundred — each to the same man. The owner was not pressing for payment. In fact, realizing that both of them were in financial difficulties, he wiped off the entire debt for the two of them. "Now, Simon, tell me, which of these men loved him the more?" The obvious answer was that he loved more who had been forgiven more.

"Correct, Simon," and Jesus pointed to the kneeling woman. "Look at this woman. When I came into your house you failed, designedly, to show me the ordinary acts of courtesy by which a host normally expresses welcome for his guest. You did not kiss me. You did not wash my feet. But how touchingly had this girl made up for your deliberate rudeness! This you have seen for yourself. So let me tell you that many sins are forgiven her because she has loved much. All she owed is forgiven and forgotten, and even if it were five times as great it would have been cancelled just the same."

Then to Mary came a word for herself, the first He had spoken to her throughout, but what a wealth of love and understanding it contained, and with what a depth of reassurance did it sink into her heart! "Your sins are forgiven," He told her. "Your faith has saved you. Go in peace."

Mary's permanent home was in the village of Bethany, where she lived with her sister Martha and her brother Lazarus. Life was quiet in this backwater place, far too dull and uninteresting at times for the spirited young girl who felt she could not exist without a nonstop program of thrills. We surmise that she had gone down to Magdala, the lively city by the sea, to find more congenial companionship.

After she had encountered Christ the facade fell away. She would never be the same again. She saw now, with a clarity that stunned and frightened her, what a hollow, aimless existence she had been leading. She had never really fulfilled herself. She now saw that no sooner was one escapade over than it was forgotten. Whatever pleasure or excitement it had given was now spent. If it was not followed at once with another, or at least with the hope or promise of another, she was plunged into bitterness and depression. There was nothing stable — no peace of mind, no power to reflect and discover what was hidden in life, what was its real purpose and explanation. Not until now had she realized how unsatisfying it all was, because only now had she taken time out to think.

It was childish, and all this time Magdalene has squandered hours and days and months and even whole years amusing herself, playing with children's toys! Christ is the light of the world; the way, the truth and the life. She came back to Bethany after that interview with Him with her whole outlook on life profoundly changed. She became more silent, more reserved, less impetuous, less insistent on having everything her own way. There was no suggestion of moroseness in all this. On the contrary, people found her much more pleasant and easier to get along with, more approachable, more ready to lend a helping hand, more controlled in temper. They marveled at the change and they were at a loss to understand how it had come about.

Bethany

Jesus, we read, "loved Martha and Mary and Lazarus their brother." He often came to see them. He was not God only but fully a man as well. He responded gratefully to the warmth and sincerity of the welcome they gave Him. It was such a relief to escape for a while from the scribes and pharisees and their hair-splitting arguments, their efforts to catch Him out, make Him contradict Himself in what He said, narrowly watching His every act to see if they could find in His most innocent gesture the wherewithal to trump up some accusation against Him. It was a tax on His powers of endurance to know that everything was being checked and tabulated and carefully registered, in the hope that it might, at some future date, supply material to show Him up in a false light.

Everything was so different in the little family at Bethany. He felt as much at home there as when He was living with His mother and Joseph in the cottage at Nazareth. Here He was genuinely loved. Here there was no danger of having His words twisted or torn from their context or His actions deliberately misconstrued.

His visit was always priority number one. The women, as their way was, thought nothing too good for Him, and it was a delight to them to prepare and serve a faultless meal. He had promised to come one evening, and this was the signal for pleasant excitement and bustle for the two sisters. He arrived. They welcomed Him, gave Him a chair and talked informally for a few minutes. Then Martha excused herself and withdrew. She had to look after the dinner. She had taken great care to have everything very *chic* so she could not afford to be too long absent from her kitchen.

And Mary? Why, Mary found her way to His feet once more, to sit there just as she had done in Simon's house at Magdala. But this time there were no tears of sorrow. All she wanted was to be near Him, to look upon Him, to listen in silence to His voice and let His words sink into the depths of her soul. Poor Mary forgot about the grand dinner, forgot about sister Martha doing all the work on her own, forgot everything except the one all-obliterating fact that it was He. Martha put up with this for a while, but after all there is a limit to what one can take. So she emerged from her kitchen and burst into the room to register a protest. "Lord," she exclaimed, "do you not care that my sister is leaving all the work to me? Please tell her come along and give me a hand with the dishes." A little domestic problem, and Jesus is being inveigled into it. What is His solution? "Martha, Martha, you are troubled and worried uselessly and about too many things. Only one thing is necessary. Mary has chosen the better part, which shall not be taken away from her." This is no condemnation of Martha. What it amounts to is: "Martha, in your great love for me you are preparing many nice things for our lunch. But actually one would be quite sufficient." St. Teresa told her nuns: "Martha is a saint, though she is not said to be a contemplative. Now what do you desire more than to be able to resemble this blessed woman who served so often to entertain Christ in her house? Had she been like Magdalene, always absorbed, there would have been no one to provide food for the divine guest."

Christ did not chide Martha merely because she gave herself to external works. No more than Vatican II censures us for engaging in the active works of the apostolate. Indeed this is understatement, for in the present condition of the Church and the world, it would be nothing short of criminal for us, priests, religious, and laity, to fold our arms and sit back and do nothing about it. What Christ did rebuke in Martha, and what the Church must do everything possible to forestall, is a pouring out of all our energy on external activities, so that they become largely a mere pandering to our love of change, noise, and natural excitement. In this there is real danger, for such unrestrained giving of ourselves to external things is bound to dry up our taste for prayer and a true interior life. Have we here the explanation of the deplorable loss of vocations among priests and religious of our day? If, because of our absorption in externals, the love of Christ wilts and dies within us, what is more easy to understand than that we seek to compensate ourselves by a ceaseless round of activities? Any loophole by which to escape from silence and stillness and prayer in depth! Life becomes a perpetual rush, largely if not wholly devoid of any supernatural motive.

This is what is implied in Our Lord's warning to Martha. One wonders if there was ever an age when it was more pressingly urgent than it has been in the Seventies. Unless the branch abide in the vine it is certain to wither and die. After that it is fit for nothing except to be cast into the fire.

Dated?

A colleague of mine and I talked together recently along these lines. He maintained that in the training given to Jesuits in the past, undue emphasis was laid on individualistic piety. What kind of spiritual books were we given to read? All of them insisted on personal holiness, on the cultivation of the spirit of prayer and sacrifice, and on the virtues of obedience, humility, charity, silence and "withdrawal from the world." Meanwhile the devil was having a field day outside. But why worry? We, fortunate people, were singularly blessed and chosen by God, secure behind our monastery walls, making steady progress in the way of perfection, while so many others were left to sink or swim in the waves.

I agreed, up to a point. Mistakes were made in the past, but is there not grave danger in this present time that what was offered as a cure may prove itself to be worse than the disease it was intended to heal? By all means let us have activity, but an activity overflowing from our own interior lives of prayer and union with God, and not substituting for it.

Nothing was farther from the wish or intention of those who gave us our spiritual training in the past than to dampen our zeal for the works of the apostolate. But heavy emphasis was laid on the fact that activity was fraught with danger — it might easily lead even to shipwreck. Therefore no one should enter upon it until he was solidly formed in the ways of prayer and union with God.

Whatever charges may be leveled against the methods of the past — and we admit that there were cases where they were justified — this much at least must be granted, that by and large those trained in the old ways stayed the course. The exodus began when the principles for genuine renewal, as laid down by Vatican II, were misinterpreted or misapplied.

The relevance of all this is by no means confined to priests and religious. It is practical for anyone seeking to exercise an apostolate that will be really effective. High tribute should be paid to great numbers of our laity who recognize the cogency of this line of argument and govern their works of zeal accordingly.

St. Thérèse of Lisieux entered Carmel when she was fifteen and died there when she was twenty-four: nine years, during which she had no direct contact with "the world." She did not go on the missions or nurse the sick or teach in school. She wrote a book, only one, and that because her prioress told her to write it. She died in obscurity. Not only is she a canonized saint, but she is proclaimed by the Church as "Patron of the Foreign Missions," on exactly the same level as St. Francis Xavier who wore himself out in working in the active apostolate. Does the moral need to be stressed? "One single act of the pure love of God," writes St. John of the Cross, "is more precious in the sight of God *and of greater service to the Church*, even though the soul appears to be doing nothing, than all these works together." He is talking about works, good in themselves, but lacking in a supernatural spirit. For good measure, here is Vatican II: "The Church today looks for a total, immediate responsiveness to God; the courageous, if sometimes faltering will, to center one's whole vision, one's whole life, on God alone." In view of all this it is highly gratifying to observe a great increase, which is still mounting, in the interest being taken in prayer today.

We have allowed ourselves to slip, almost unnoticed, into a lengthy digression, due to the importance of the subject. We apologize to our readers and hasten now to return with them to Martha and Mary.

Back To Bethany

The house at Bethany was a rendezvous for Christ and His friends. It seems likely that He may have slept there on the Wednesday night preceding the Passion. Mary, His mother, may have lodged there too. Jesus went out in the late evening of Holy Thursday and did not return. It was a night of grave anxiety for the little group He had left behind. The city was full of men who hated Him and wanted to kill Him. His mother and the two sisters and Lazarus must have felt uneasy. They assumed He had gone to celebrate the pasch, but it was now long after the hour for that and still there was no sign of His return. The four of them sat there in the kitchen. For the most part they sat in silence. Conversation was unnecessary. Each of them knew where the thoughts of the others lay. They prayed. An occasional footstep outside in the street and they strained their ears. It seemed to be drawing near the house. They hoped it might be He. But the traveler, whoever he was, did not halt or knock at the door. He moved on. The sound of the footfall gradually died away, and the little company sank back again into their agony of suspense.

After that night — the events of which we have tried to reconstruct by what we hope was a legitimate use of the imagination — Scripture is silent about Magdalene until it tells us she was with Our Lady at Calvary. But it does seem very reasonable to assume that she went out into the street soon after dawn on the Friday morning, no longer able to endure the state of anxiety and uncertainty. Everything we know of her character, her ardent nature, her consuming love of Christ, her torture of mind for His safety, almost forces us to the conclusion that she mingled with the crowds outside the house of Caiaphas during the trial, that she joined in the procession from Caiaphas to Pilate and from Pilate to Herod and back again.

So she would have seen Christ standing on the balcony of Pilate's palace, bleeding and crowned with thorns after the scourging. She might even have listened to the swish of the lashes as they fell upon Him at the pillar. She heard the inane cries of the mob demanding that He be crucified. She saw Barabbas preferred before Him. She was shocked to learn that the Jews were prepared to accept the hated Roman for their king but not Jesus of Nazareth. Pilate said: "Behold the man!" The crowd insisted that He should be crucified. Pilate gave sentence and Christ was led forth. Magdalene was there, absorbing every detail.

Did Mary, the mother of Jesus, accompany her? Undoubtedly. It is inconceivable that she could have been anywhere else. "O all ye who pass by this wayside, attend and see if there be any sorrow like my sorrow." Christ had lifted Magdalene up out of the welter of sin and had placed her side-by-side with another Mary. The erstwhile sinful woman and the ever-spotless virgin-mother became inseparable companions. Only a divine lover could forgive like that.

Then a member of the council arrived, an upright and virtuous man named Joseph. He had not consented to what the others had planned and carried out. He came from Arimathea, a Jewish town, and he lived in the hope of seeing the kingdom of God. This man went to Pilate and asked for the body of Jesus. He helped to take it down from the cross; he wrapped it in a shroud; he placed it in a tomb hewn in stone in which no one had yet been laid. The whole group had to leave hurriedly, for it was preparation day and the sabbath was imminent.

Christ had said: "Destroy this temple and in three days I will rebuild it." His enemies affected to think He was speaking of the material temple in which they were standing. Actually he was referring to His own body. That they knew this quite well is clearly shown by the request they made to Pilate immediately after the funeral. "We have remembered," they told him, "that the seducer said while he was yet alive that he would rise again the third day. Command, then, that the tomb be guarded for three days, lest his followers come and steal the body and say he is risen, and the last error be worse than the first." Pilate did so.

"Meantime the women, who had come from Galilee with Jesus ... had taken note of the tomb and the position of the body. Then they returned and prepared spices and ointments, and on the sabbath day they rested, as the law required." The precautions taken to guard the tomb proved unavailing. Jesus rose "according to the Scriptures." He showed Himself alive, to several persons and many times over. One of the first to see Him was Magdalene, the woman who was a sinner, out of whom He had expelled seven devils. As we shall see, He came to Mary, His mother, first of all.

Miriam!

Early in the grey dawn, when the Sabbath was ended, Magdalene was on her way to the graveyard. She stood and stared in amazement at what she saw. The guards were lying flat on the ground, to all appearances motionless in death. The great stone, which had been placed at the opening of the sepulcher, had been rolled back. The girl took her courage in her hands, walked timidly up to the opening and looked strainingly inside. As yet there was not much light, but it was bright enough to convince her that the grave was empty. Incredulous, she peered again and again, hoping she was wrong, hoping she might see more clearly as the morning advanced. No. There was no mistake. Whatever had happened to the body of Jesus, it most certainly was not there. A shattering truth.

She remained standing there beside the empty tomb, not knowing what to do. By a sudden impulse she decided to go back to the city and tell the others of her amazing discovery. "She ran away and came to Simon Peter and to the other disciple whom Jesus loved. 'The Lord has been taken out of the

tomb,' she said, 'and we do not know where he has been laid.' "
The first reaction of the two men is to suspect that the poor girl's
mind has been deranged as a result of all her grief and strain over
the past three days. Indeed till even late that afternoon, to some
of Christ's men friends the Resurrection seemed to be an idle tale,
which they attributed to the overwrought imaginations of these
highly emotional women. They did not think it worthwhile
even to go out to the grave and see for themselves.

It was not the first time in history that credulous women
got the story right — nor will it be the last — while the hardheaded, commonsense, practical men were wide of the mark.

Peter and John, however, decided to go and investigate
Magdalene's extraordinary tale. Magdalene would surely have
spoken about her discovery to Our Lady, to Martha and to Laza-
rus. She would have relayed the account for the other apostles.
These would have taken some time, during which Peter and
John could have rejoined them and confirmed that the tomb was
empty. We are not told that Christ's mother went to the grave.
The explanation for this, suggested by the late Father Michael
Egan, S.J., is that her Son had already appeared to her and
shown Himself to her in the glory of His Resurrection.

But Magdalene is still disconsolate. Guided by love more
than by cold reason, she returns to the grave. Nothing has
changed since her previous visit except that there is now full
daylight to reassure her *He* is not there.

Where is she to turn? Who is there to tell her what has happened, and, more urgent still, where was the body? Presently a
shadow falls across her path and she hears a footstep. Here is a
man who might be the caretaker. "Sir," she says, "if you know
where they have put him, please tell me where and I will take
him away."

This is the language of the "maddening love" spoken of
elsewhere. So absorbed is her mind with the thought of Jesus
that she does not even mention Him by name. Then there is the
naive suggestion that she should take Him away. Just imagine

this woman struggling under the weight of His dead body. And where did she propose to place Him? All these commonsense questions never occurred to her. Love is like that.

The dramatic moment has come. The "gardener" speaks one single word and instantly the light of recognition leaps into her eyes. She knows the sound of that voice so well that mistake is impossible. As if to preclude all possibility of error He employs the more familiar form of her name, by which He had addressed her many times since first they met in the house of Simon at Magdala. "Miriam?" At once she is back in her privileged place at His feet, exclaiming "Rabboni!" — a word expressing much more reverence than the more common one, which was "Rabbi." Moreover, its use was almost exclusively reserved for God.

She keeps on holding His feet as though fearful He might go as suddenly as He had come. But He reassures her. "I am not yet ascended to my Father. You will see me again. Go and find my brothers and say to them: 'I ascend to my Father and your Father; to my God and to your God.'" So Magdalene went and told the disciples. To them she brought Christ back. She will help us in our task to do the same.

PETER

It is easy and common enough to accuse Peter of cowardice, though the proofs, we suggest, are not convincing. No emphasis is thrown on his courage. It generally passes unnoticed, denied or forgotten, whereas a little careful and prayerful reading of his story reveals clearly a man who, if we allow for human weaknesses, is capable of rising up to great heights of heroism. We propose in this chapter first to follow the line of thought which those persons pursue who think Peter was a weakling and, after that, to take a look at their arguments and see if they are really quite valid.

At the last supper Peter had made a great show of bravery and loyalty to Christ. Our Lord had warned him and the rest of the group that on this very night they would all abandon Him in His hour of need. "You will all lose faith in me this very night," He said, "for the scripture says: 'I will strike the shepherd and the sheep of the flock shall be scattered.' " At once Peter jumps to his feet to make a protest. This is not going to happen. The other eleven? Well, for them he could not speak. But about this much at least he was certain, that the Lord could depend on Peter. "Even if I were to die with you, Lord, I would never disown you."

Christ insists. "This very night, Peter, before the cock crows, you will have denied me three times." Peter, full of confidence in himself, refuses to be convinced. He goes to the length of countering Christ's warning with a flat contradiction. There must be a mistake somewhere. Whatever ominous events are brooding, whatever tests and trials are awaiting them tonight, Peter will take them in his stride. The Master and the brethren will see. Whatever ontoward may be lying ahead in the immediate future, they will all be compelled to confess that Peter has come through without swerving an inch from his loyalty to Christ. A few hours and they will see this. "Lord, I am ready to go with you to prison and to death." "And in like manner spoke all the disciples." Fine high-sounding words, which cost little. Peter knows no fear till real danger appears.

The scene now shifts to the barrackyard outside the house of Caiaphas, the high priest. After the meal Jesus had gone with, this time, eleven of His apostles to spend some time in prayer, as was His custom, in the garden of Gethsemani. He sweated blood that night during His vigil, as He knelt under the olive trees in the broken rays of the moonlight. He was terrified at the prospect of the ordeal He had to face. He shuddered in horror and was filled with loathing at the vision of sin He must expiate. Human He was, like ourselves, and in His hour of anguish He sought some human consolation from His friends. He had brought Peter and James and John with Him to support Him, asking them to watch and pray with Him. He sought them out now only to discover that they were fast asleep. "Their eyes were heavy, and they did not know what to say to him" (Mark 14:40).

Is this the sort of stuff from which courage is made?

All three of them had failed Him, but Peter's failure is the most glaring in view of the fact that he had boasted more arrogantly than the others and was not shaken in his self-confidence even by Christ's own weighty words of warning. True, when a horde of armed soldiers came on the scene at the end of the prayer of Christ, stating that they had been commissioned to arrest Him, Peter leaped to His assistance. He drew his sword to defend his Lord and rescue Him from the hands of His enemies, who were "a large number of men, armed with swords and clubs." Peter struck at the servant of the high priest and cut off his right ear. This sudden blazing up of showmanship, which was quite in accord with Peter's impetuous character, fizzled out as quickly as it had arisen, and the valiant Peter, fearful of the consequences to himself, pushed his sword back into its scabbard and ran for his life. They all ran with him, thoroughly scared, while the soldiers proceeded to handcuff their prisoner and lead him away. What a fine demonstration they gave that night — Peter and the rest of them — of loyalty and bravery!

Three Times

That episode is over now. The armed forces had an easy task. They had got the man they were sent to fetch. There was no further opposition after Peter's futile interference. They had tied the hands of Jesus and led Him from the garden through the city streets and brought Him to the house of Annas, father-in-law to the high priest Caiaphas. Annas was a crafty, scheming old man who probably had been at the back of the plans to seize Jesus. The prisoner was brought to him now so that he might gloat over the capture that had at last been achieved. Annas was a vicious and influential old scoundrel, who although now holding no official position, was in fact the real power behind the throne. His vanity had to be flattered. Caiaphas, who actually held the reins of government in his hands, would not dare to drive in any direction without first consulting the old man and securing his approval.

Annas is supremely content. He has feasted his eyes on his victim, swearing under his breath that nothing but death will rescue Him from their clutches. He signals to the soldiers to take Him off, and Jesus is led to the courtyard outside the palace of Caiaphas, the high priest. A stone staircase reaches from the ground floor to the rooms overhead. In one of these judge and jury are seated — Caiaphas and the members of the council, or sanhedrin — with all preparations made to conduct the trial of Jesus of Nazareth. Down below the soldiers indicate to the prisoner that he is to climb that stair. He obeys. He walks into the room on top and stands, with his hands still tied in front, to answer the charges brought against him. What follows is one of the most galling travesties of justice in the history of the human race.

It is a cold night, and the attendants have lighted a fire in the courtyard downstairs. While the trial is proceeding up above, soldiers and servants and loiterers have gathered here to warm themselves and have a chat, some of them regaling themselves from time to time with a draught from the bottles hanging from their belts. They discuss the events of the evening, especially the prisoner, this meddlesome Jesus of Nazareth and the crazy notion he had about himself that he was king of the Jews. Tomorrow will put an end to his pretensions. He does not stand a chance against the cunning old Annas — or Caiaphas, who, as everyone knows, is just a tool in Annas' hands.

And of all people, who is right in the midst of the group but Simon Peter, squatting there on his heels in oriental fashion, stretching out his hands to the comforting warmth of the fire! Those who would have us believe that he was a coward would tell us that his face was ashen-white with terror and his heart thumping within him lest he be recognized and questioned and accused.

After running away from the garden with the others Peter had retraced his steps. He got as far as the gate of the courtyard. It was locked. But another disciple came to his rescue and asked the portress to open it for him. It is generally taken for granted that this other disciple was John, although there are scholars who consider this unlikely. They think that it was some more influential person like Nicodemus or Joseph of Arimathea. What concerns us more is that Peter, somehow, did gain admission and mingled with those warming themselves at the fire. He wanted to see the end of this business. He would follow Jesus from "afar off," at a safe distance, so as not to compromise himself. It was easy to brag at the supper table, but this courtyard and this mob presented a very different picture. This time there was real danger and real risk, and a man must be sensible and cautious and take no chances.

Now was that not brave of him? Worse is to follow. As he

stands or squats there at the fire he begins to realize what a fool he has been. Better never to have come back! Why did he not remain with the rest of the brethren in safety, probably with their devoted friends in Bethany. Instead, impulsive as always, he has rushed back into the jaws of danger. Such a glaring mistake, more especially as at this stage there is absolutely nothing he can do to help his Master. Better slip unobtrusively away from this mob at the fire and make his escape quietly while there is time and opportunity. Misery is eating into his soul.

His thoughts are rudely interrupted. Clear and loud, pitched high above the coarse mutterings of the men, rings out the shrill note of a girl's voice. "Why," she cries, "here is one of the very men we have been talking about." And she leans forward to scrutinize his features in the glare of the fire. "This is a friend of the Nazarene. He drew a sword to defend him." And she points an accusing finger in the direction of the apostle. Peter rises hastily, stands still, with head and shoulders bent slightly forward, completely taken by surprise and undecided what to do. For one agonizing moment, fear for himself and love and loyalty for Jesus have a struggle in his heart. The eyes of all are fixed on him. Some jostle one another in the effort to secure a better view.

The situation is beginning to look very ugly. With a gesture of pretended anger and indignation to cloak over his inward terror, Peter scowls at them and shouts at the girl: "I have no idea of what you are talking about. Never saw the man, never met him, in my whole life!"

The lie stuck in his throat. His conscience protested at once and refused to be silenced. He shuffled away from them, glaring contemptuously on them, simulating scorn and fury and resenting the suggestion that he had any associations with Jesus of Nazareth.

He moved over toward the archway, possibly with the scheme to escape through the gate leading into the street outside. Safety awaited him there and deliverance from any further questionings or accusations. But the fates were against him. The portress had locked the gate while the trial of Christ was proceeding.

Peter finds himself a prisoner. What to do? To ask the girl to let him out might easily provoke further suspicions, so once more he starts to walk about aimlessly, at a loss to know what to do or where to turn.

He did not have much time to decide. Another maid espied him and remembered vaguely having seen him somewhere before. Where was it? Perhaps she had been close to him in the city in the great procession through the streets last Sunday. If so she had had opportunity to get a good look at him then so she is now convinced that it must be the same man. She is quick to tell her friends. "You see this fellow? I know him well. I saw him before. He is one of the friends of the Nazarene."

Another torrent of fury sweeps over the soul of Simon Peter. Why can these busybody women not mind their own business? This featherheaded girl by her thoughtlessness has driven him into a tight corner. He must seize upon the first loophole to extricate himself. "It's a lie," he tells her. His denial is met with a giggle from the maid, which tells Peter and everyone else who hears it that she knows what she is talking about. This intruder, with a glib lie so ready on his tongue, is probably up to no good.

Poor Peter, and his troubles are not over yet. Disconsolate, he saunters back to the fire and the company there, but this time with a new approach. This time he will brazen the thing out. He will join in their conversation, start asking questions about the prisoner and thus create the impression that he did not know Him before and would welcome some information about Him. A fatal step, for no sooner has he opened his mouth to speak than his hearers recognize his Galilean accent. They could not be mistaken. It was notorious. So harsh and unpleasant that no Galilean was allowed to pronounce the blessing at a Jewish service in the synagogue.

So they called his bluff straightaway. Was he such a knave or fool, they wanted to know, as to imagine they did not sense what lay behind his apparently innocent questions about Jesus? "Why, even your very accent betrays you that you are a Galilean." Peter, this time really enraged, began to curse and to swear that he did not know Christ.

"The Lord, Turning . . ."

But at that moment all eyes are suddenly taken off Peter. His vehement protests are ignored. The debate ends unexpectedly. Something far more interesting has caught the attention of the crowd. Peter follows their gaze and what he sees keeps him rooted to the spot.

The first trial of the prisoner is ended. They see Jesus coming out of the high priest's room and standing for a moment at the top of the flight of stairs leading down into the courtyard. A soldier nudges Him rudely, indicating that He is to go on ahead. Jesus begins the descent, step by step. He cannot gather in His cloak around Him, and if there is a bannister He cannot avail of it, for His hands remain still tied together all this time. Peter is mesmerized. Christ has reached the last step of the stairs and has walked on to the floor of the courtyard. They have come very close to each other now. Christ passes him by.

Not a word did he speak. Not a sign of recognition did He show lest He should give Peter away. But "the Lord, turning, looked at Peter." There was no anger, no rebuke, no censure in that look; only a love that persisted still, only pity and pardon and understanding and mercy.

"The Lord, turning, looked at Peter." There is a whole world of pathos in the evangelist's simple sentence. That look seemed to choke Peter's heart with sorrow. It pierced his soul like a two-edged sword. Light shone from those eyes and penetrated into the innermost depths of that soul, like a ray of sunshine breaking through the darkness of the clouds. It was all over in a few seconds, but it had lasted long enough to reveal the whole horrible truth to the man who had called himself the friend of Christ and had just now cursed and sworn that he never knew Him.

Peter, who had been so loud in acclaiming his love and loyalty. Peter, who had left all things to follow Christ. Peter, for whom the Lord had prayed especially that his faith might not fail. Peter, whom Christ had commissioned to confirm his brethren, to be their model and support. Peter, to whom the promise had been made that he was to be the rock upon which the Church of God would rest securely. Peter had denied Christ — three times over did he deny Him — and had confirmed his denials and his betrayal with oaths and curses!

All Christ's lovable ways come flooding into his mind — His patience, His thoughtfulness, His gentleness combined with indomitable strength — more attractive now than ever in the light of Peter's fall. Echoes start up suddenly in the man's tortured brain: "Even though all should deny you . . .," "I am ready to go with you to prison and to death . . .," "*I* will never be scandalized . . ." and "the Lord turning, looked at Peter. . . ." The remorse of it all! Such a friend betrayed! And betrayed by such an apostle! And betrayed for such a reason — because he was afraid of the jibes of a frivolous little servant maid! Then the cock crowed, and "Peter remembered what Jesus had spoken: 'Before the cock crows, you will deny me three times.' And going out, he wept bitterly" — so bitterly and so long, tradition tells us, that the tears cut furrows into his cheeks.

This crowing of the cock confronts us with a little problem. Does it seem likely that there was a poultry farm situated in the center of the city and within the precincts of the high priest's house! Actually there was a rule forbidding this, because it was considered that the presence of the poultry would defile the holy places. What, then, did Peter hear? The Romans and the Jews divided the night into four periods of equal duration, each lasting three hours, from six in the evening till six in the morning. Each new period was announced by a trumpet call, sounded from the roof of the Palace Antonia and audible all over the city. The events we have just been considering would have coincided in time with the change of the guard. The Latin word indicating this change was *gallicinium,* which in English would be rendered "cock-crow."

Was this what Peter heard when he stood motionless, dazed and heartbroken after his triple denial of Christ? The theory is attractive, and, perhaps, more plausible than the more commonly accepted one.

The Courage of Peter

Our presentation of the story of Peter so far is, in the main, the one given by those who consider him to be a coward. But he was nothing of the kind. This is not to say he can be exonerated as completely as some writers would maintain. "I, for one," writes a Methodist clergyman, "do not believe that Peter denied Jesus. I think Peter was seeking information. As many another has done in a great cause, before and since, he was playing the part of a spy. ... However he blundered, his conscience did not hold him guilty of anything except losing his head in a misguided attempt to serve his Master." We feel compelled to call this view *naive.* Of course Peter sinned. Otherwise why did Christ warn him and foretell his three denials? Why did He pray for Peter especially? Why did He look upon him with sorrow after Peter's sin? And why did Peter go out into the dark and weep bitterly? However much we love Peter and however much we would wish to excuse him, it seems clear that in the interests of truth we must reluctantly admit that he failed deplorably. But this is not to say he was a coward. When he told Christ that he was ready to go with Him to prison and to death, he spoke from the fullness of his heart and meant every word he said. What followed afterward, and what seems to contradict this, was the outcome, not of cowardice but of deep personal love of Christ, anxiety about what might befall Him, and a restless urge to be close to Him in case there was need or opportunity to defend or rescue him.

No one can deny that it took a lot of courage for one single man to draw his sword and face a platoon of armed soldiers. Peter did just that. He risked his life and proved he was ready to give for Christ that proof of love greater than which no man has, that a man lay down his life for his friends. He was the only apostle on that night who tried to prove his love by deeds as well as by words. If he put back his sword into its place he did so in obedience to a definite order from his Master. Otherwise he might well have been killed that night if a skirmish had ensued — as was likely enough to happen. He must have realized the serious risk he was taking, but brave soldier and lover of Christ that he was, he did not count the cost.

Capital is often made of the fact that when Peter and the others saw Jesus bound and a prisoner, they panicked and "all leaving him, fled away." It is by no means certain that this was cowardice. Just consider the circumstances. First of all, the entire group was perfectly well aware that they had nothing whatever to fear for their personal safety. Only one man was wanted, and for his arrest only did the soldiers hold a writ. They had got their man, and they did not have the slightest interest in his followers, who they were or what they did. Nothing concerned them except to execute the orders given, and these orders referred to Jesus whom they were now leading back to the city. The rest of the group might do exactly as they pleased and remain unmolested, provided they made no disturbance. They knew that perfectly well, so they had no grounds for fear. A foolish theory advanced by some modern pedants is that they were so terrified that they ran away, not only from the garden, but from Jerusalem itself, all the way back to Galilee, leaving their friends and womenfolk and property behind them. They could not escape quickly enough! The idea underlying this fantastic tale is to have the disciples out of the way before Sunday and thus make Christ's resurrection less plausible.

It is true that "the disciples, all leaving him, fled away." But when we come to consider this more deeply we have to ask what else could they have done? They found themselves in a situation entirely without precedent in all their dealings with Our Lord, and they were, frankly, completely at a loss to know how to handle it. First of all the fact was staring them in the face that to resist by force would be suicidal. What chance had eleven poor inexperienced men against the number, vast by comparison, of disciplined, thoroughly trained Roman military men? And, even if they were ready to fight, there was the further consideration that Christ clearly was opposed to violence and had, indeed, peremptorily forbidden it. "Put back your sword," He had told Peter, adding that if he so willed all he had to do was call on His Father for twelve legions of angels to protect Him.

This very statement is a further proof that they were not cowards. Never before had they seen Christ as they saw Him now — bound and a prisoner. On other occasions, before "His hour" had come, efforts to take Him failed. He simply walked through or disappeared mysteriously. What was to prevent His doing the same now? Newman was to write, in a different context, about "Omnipotence in Bonds." These men witnessed it. They were bewildered. They could not adjust their minds to it. Had they remembered the words of the prophet, the position might have been clarified for them. "He was offered because it was his own will, and he opened not his mouth" (Isaiah 53:7).

In view of all this, it seems hardly fair to them to accuse them of cowardice.

Is Peter an Exception?

Why did Peter come back so soon and manage to gain admittance into the courtyard while the trial of Christ was going on upstairs? By no stretch of the imagination could anyone in his senses construe this as the act of a coward. If Peter was a coward he would have kept at a safe distance, well removed from

Christ's enemies, avoiding any risk of injury to himself. He would have been congratulating himself on getting away so successfully. He would have taken good care to lie low and await developments and only then decide on what his policy should be.

But that was not Peter. The affection he had for Christ was like a magnet drawing him irresistibly. He cannot but wonder what is going to happen; he must go and find out for himself. Why, then, did he deny Christ three times? The motive here was fear indeed, but not fear for himself. He was terrified lest, if he admitted to being a friend of the Nazarene he would be summarily ejected from the place, and with all the ardor of his great heart he wanted to stay.

That was why he felt no great compunction about applying a false principle — to be fathered on the Jesuits at a much later day — that the end justifies the means. He was wrong. He told a deliberate lie, and a lie is always a sin. Had he been summoned as a witness at the subsequent trial of Jesus, we cannot doubt that he would have given his testimony fearlessly, proclaiming in front of the whole assembly of judge and jury that Christ is the Son of the living God who is come into this world. Actually he would one day make that very statement and die rather than take back a word of it.

Our Lord foretold this: "When you were younger, Peter, you put on your own belt and walked where you liked. But when you grow old you will stretch out your hands and somebody else will put a belt around you and take you where you would rather not go" (John 21:18). In these words Christ indicated by what sort of death Peter would glorify God. Like Christ Peter died nailed to a cross. But he deemed himself unworthy of this and asked, as a last request, that he be fastened to his cross with his head downwards.

Because pride is so deeply rooted in us, we find it difficult to admit our faults and shortcomings. We do our best to conceal them, excuse them, sometimes even to try to pass them off as virtues. We are resentful if another points them out, no matter how tactfully, no matter what high motives may inspire him. A confirmed alcoholic finds it difficult to stand up before twelve or fifteen men with the same problem as himself and say to them boldly, "I am an alcoholic." The day he succeeds in doing so he has taken the first step in the direction of his complete cure.

A man in the dock, on trial for murder or embezzling large sums of money, will at times deny the charge although he is perfectly well aware that it is true. He will swear on oath he is innocent and will invent stories to prove it. He will call on the God of truth to witness to the falsehood, rating lightly this additional appalling crime of perjury piled up on his previous record of wickedness.

If Peter was a coward he would have taken steps to secure that the story of his weakness would never have leaked out. This would have been easy because no one knew about it, and so people would think none the worse of him for it. All he had to do was keep his mouth closed, and he could have persuaded himself that as chief pastor of Christ's flock, he owed this secrecy to upholding the dignity of his office. He could not afford to lose prestige by letting it be known that he had denied Christ three times, and with oaths and curses thrown in for good measure.

That seemed to make sense. But actually what did he do? St. Mark is the writer to whom we are indebted for the full account of the story. Now it is historically proved that what Mark did, for the most part, was to preserve and transcribe what he had heard from Peter's preaching. So we can fairly conclude that it was Peter himself who gave to the world for all time, his detailed account of his sin and weakness, his vain boasting, his lies, the triple denial. We would never have heard a word about it except for him. Far from suppressing it, he broadcast it to the ends of the earth. Would you call a man like that a coward?

In many parts of the world today people are drawing courage from the example of Matt Talbot, the Dublin workman who was a convert from alcoholism. He is now, thank God, the "Venerable Matthew," and we are now permitted to hope that one day he will be both beatified and canonized. At one time he would go to the lengths of taking off his shoes and pawning them to get money for drink. He went to confession one night, took the pledge against drink for life, and never looked back. For the first four months he tells us he went through hell!

There is a parallel between St. Peter and the Venerable Matthew Talbot. Both sinned and both repented. Both tell us that "forgiven sin is no bar to intimacy with Jesus." This is true, but it is understatement. Forgiven sin can be a most powerful incentive to a life of heroic sanctity. Peter never knew Christ so well as after he had hurt Him. It was then, most of all, that he came to understand His changeless love, His compassion, His readiness to begin all over again as if nothing had happened.

JUDAS

Is Judas in hell? Who can say? I know a priest who prays for Judas by name in nearly every Mass he celebrates. That same priest asks people to commend Judas to God in their prayers and also to remember people like Hitler, Stalin, Lenin, and Nero. We feel justified in at least fostering a strong hope that the traitor apostle did indeed repent of his crime from his heart, that he was forgiven and is now in heaven. We have to admit, I suppose, that a black enough case could be made out against him. Still, it is also true that:

> "There's a wideness in God's mercy like the wideness of the sea.
> There's a kindness in his justice which is more than clemency.
> For the love of God is broader than the measure of man's mind,
> And the heart of the Eternal is most wonderfully kind.
> But we make his love too narrow with false limits of our own,
> And we multiply his strictness with a zeal he will not own . . ." (Father Faber).

One has heard the sin of Judas described as "the blackest crime that ever stained the scrolls of history." Perhaps that is true. But if it is and if Judas is saved, his salvation will attest for all eternity and in quite a unique manner to the infinite mercy of God. This, too, can be said, and with deep conviction — that if there was a way possible to find by which to save him, short of forcing his free will, God would unquestionably have found it. "I desire not the death of the sinner but that he should be converted and live" (Ezekiel 33:11). We know, too, the kindness and patience and affection with which Christ treated His renegade apostle. We remember the exquisite tact with which He shielded his reputation, giving no hint to the other apostles of the foul plan Judas had formed in his heart.

All through the entire sad story, right up to the very moment of that fatal kiss, it is clear that Christ is more concerned about the injury Judas is doing to Judas than He is about the hurt to Himself.

Despair

If Judas is in hell, why is he there? If we answer without reflecting, we shall probably say because he betrayed Christ, because he made a blood bargain with men who hated Him, because he took their money from them, because he conducted the soldiers to a spot where they could arrest Christ with impunity, and finally and most of all, because he indicated His identity by kissing Him. A terrifying catalogue of crimes, no doubt. But no one of them, nor all of them combined, however contemptible they might be and however gravely sinful, need necessarily have climaxed with eternity in hell for the man who did them. What the unfortunate Judas forgot, if he had ever known it, was that there is no sin, no matter how heinous, no matter how often repeated, that God is not most willing and eager to forgive if only He finds true repentance.

Judas was haunted by the remembrance that in the particular crime committed by him there was a distinctive malice that placed it in a category all its own. How, then, could *he* expect to be forgiven? Any other sin, yes. Any other person sinning and he could admit that there were valid reasons to hope for forgiveness. But not the sin of the Iscariot! "*My* sin," he kept telling himself, "is greater than that I should hope for pardon." Judas could not bring himself to believe that the infinite ocean of God's mercy and love was wide enough and deep enough to wash away *his* particular sin. So he abandoned himself to despair in spite of the Master's obvious anxiety to draw him back from the abyss. If Judas is in hell the reason, primarily, is not that he sold Christ for money, but that he tied the hands of the omnipotent lover. What can even God do in face of such obstinacy? If right to the very end Judas persists in clapping his hands over his ears to shut off the message of mercy and hope, if to the very end he closes his eyes and refuses to look with sorrow into the loving eyes of Christ, what option does he leave to Christ except to let him go his way.

There is no sin but Christ has the power and the desire to forgive it, provided He meets with genuine repentance. That is the one essential condition. In the whole gospel you cannot find a single instance where He is hard on a sinner who comes to Him in that spirit. Not even one case. The same divine message re-echoes every time: "Be of good heart, son; your sins are forgiven" (Matthew 9:2).

Suppose

At this point may I please be allowed to make two suppositions? Suppose we had been down there in the garden of Gethsemani on that Holy Thursday night. Christ has finished His prayer. He moves out from under the shadow of the olive trees and steps into the open space, which is flooded with moonlight. His enemies are moving stealthily towards Him, carefully briefed in advance by Judas, who walks in front. "Whoever I shall kiss, that is he. Hold him fast." As we watch, we see him coming up to Jesus, putting his arms around Him and kissing Him on the cheek. That kiss has ever since stood out in the minds of men as being the symbol for all that is basest and most degrading in human friendship. "And he kissed him." This is a form of greeting or farewell usually given only where there is bond of intimate friendship. It is worthwhile noting that it caused no surprise to the other apostles. Apparently they took it for granted. Apparently it was what Judas ordinarily did whenever he came or went. What a contemptible device to try to cover up his crime by such base hypocrisy!

This is the point at which our first supposition enters. We can recall the reactions of people to Pope Paul's dramatic gesture about two years ago. At the end of a function, in sight of a dense crowd, he removed the miter from his head, handed it to an attendant, went down on his knees and bent to kiss both feet of the Orthodox Patriarch. The spectators were speechless with amazement and admiration. This was something unprecedented in history.

Now suppose Judas did something like that in the garden on Holy Thursday night. Suppose that, after he had kissed Jesus, he was at once seized by remorse and shame and sorrow as the enormity of the crime he has committed begins to dawn upon his mind. The ingratitude, cruelty, the galling injustice, the sweetness and gentleness of Christ's reactions — all these come crowding in upon him and he staggers under the crushing load. He is sickened with loathing for the whole miserable business.

He loosens his hold upon Jesus, moves back a step or two, tries to steady himself after the impact of such a shattering experience. Then, as we continue to look, we see Judas falling down on his knees in front of Christ. He joins his hands palm to palm in reverence and then extends both arms full, in the attitude of a humble supplicant. We listen breathlessly while, from the bottom of his heart, he pours out a prayer that electrifies the whole atmosphere. "God," he says, "be merciful to me, a sinner." The prayer is said slowly, with great deliberation, each phrase being given its full emphasis. Impossible to doubt the sincerity of this man's sorrow. There he kneels in shame and grief for what he has done, longing for the word from Christ that he may hope for pardon.

And the response of Jesus, what is it? He moves a step forward, bends down over the weeping apostle, rests His hands on his bowed head and speaks the words of absolution. "Be of good heart, son; your sins are forgiven."

What a profoundly moving scene that would have been! What hope it would have kindled in the hearts of us sinners, filling us with courage to return to Him after we had sinned! What a thrilling chapter it would add to the volume containing the story of the mercy of God!

But the tragedy is that that chapter was never written. Unwritten it must remain because Judas remained obdurate. You have sat, perhaps, by the seashore on a summer evening and looked out on the vast expanse of ocean — a reminder of the eternity and immensity of God. A large jutting piece of rock protrudes out of the water a few hundred yards away. With unfailing regularity the sea moves in and moves out. For a while the rock is lost to view, completely covered over by the incoming tide. But only for a while. As the waves move back and return to the ocean, the rock reappears, still hard and unrelenting, still unaffected by the contact repeatedly made. This has been going on for centuries, and still the rock abides and endures.

The waves of divine mercy and grace were surging all around the heart of Judas on that fateful Holy Thursday night in Gethsemani. We would wish to think they penetrated, and perhaps they did. But the evidence is against us. Judas, coarsened by his sin, remained impervious and obdurate. "*My* sin is too great that I should hope for pardon." The waters receded and left him just as they had found him.

Judas, a Saint?

Our story is only a supposition, of course, a mere figment of the imagination. Had it really happened, had Judas really repented, how would the story end? Judas might well have become another saint like Peter. God's priests down through the years might have offered the sacrifice of the Mass, thousands of times over, in honor of *Saint* Judas Iscariot, if only the traitor had thrown himself on the mercy of God.

Christ is prepared to forgive till seventy times seven times. There is not one instance in the whole gospel where He shows harshness to a sinner who repents sincerely, no matter what he has done. The temptation is strong to enlarge on this statement by citing case after case, but this would need a long digression we must avoid. Judas had witnessed this mercy in most, perhaps in all, the instances recorded in the gospels. Over his soul the waves had flowed, only to leave him unchanged when they receded.

Now for our second supposition. This time we are out on Calvary with the crowds who have gathered to witness the death of Christ. Some look on callously, not interested; they have seen this sort of thing before and have become inured. Others are aggressive and insulting and they point the finger of scorn at the dying man, defying Him to come down from the cross if He can. His mother is there too, and John and Magdalene, and a handful of others who had remained loyal to Him to the end.

A stranger arrives. He elbows his way through, his mind made up that no one is going to prevent him getting very close to the dying Christ. There he stands, fascinated, with eyes for nobody but that criminal on his cross. Look well at him. Yes. There is no doubt. This is Judas the Iscariot, who sold Jesus for a handful of money; who betrayed him with a kiss and is therefore largely responsible for the appalling spectacle he sees here. Overpowered by the sight, he falls on his knees beside Magdalene at the foot of the cross, a second repentant sinner.

With both hands firmly clutching the upright beam, Judas lifts up his eyes and gazes into the face of Christ. Christ opens His eyes, weighed down as they are with blood and spittle, and sees him there. No one stirs. The silence is tense. Everyone feels compelled to look and listen, whether understanding the mysterious significance of the incident or not. Judas breaks the silence.

In a voice hoarse with emotion he prays the prayer of a repentant sinner: "Lord, if you will, you can make me clean." Jesus spoke seven words on the cross, concerning which we shall have more to say in another place. Had Judas uttered that prayer for forgiveness, there would have been eight words, not seven, and the last word would have brought back the sunshine into the darkened heart of the traitor apostle. The wondering multitude would have heard it. We hear it now. "Be of good heart, son; your sins are forgiven. I *do* will it. Be made clean."

Another extraordinarily affecting scene. The calamity is that it never happened. Judas took a halter, hanged himself and died, because he persisted in persuading himself that his particular sin could not be forgiven. This was the climax of his despair.

Resumé

Earlier in the evening of that eventful Holy Thursday Judas had sat with Christ and the other eleven at the supper table. At this stage he is definitely odd man out. He does not belong here anymore. He is carrying, hidden in the recesses of his heart, a horrible secret that irritates like a festering sore. A hardheaded, down-to-earth man of the world, he is disappointed with Christ. He is disillusioned. Everything had looked so promising three years ago when first he had joined this group. The name of Christ was on everyone's lips. The whole countryside was stirred as soon as word got around that Jesus of Nazareth was passing by. Thousands followed after him for whole days at a stretch, even far away into the desert, forgetting their food and their drink and sleep, wanting only to be with him.

A rumor was floating about that he had come to restore freedom and independence to Israel, to throw off the hated Roman yoke and set up a kingdom of his own. This pleased Judas. If there was any truth in the rumor he would be keen to stand well with Jesus, for he was an ambitious man, thirsting for power and by no means uninterested in money and high finance.

He saw himself fitting perfectly into Christ's scheme of things. There was no denying that the prophet had marvelous power to sway whole multitudes with his word. With the touch of his hand he cleansed lepers, gave sight to the blind and hearing to the deaf. A word from him was enough to quell a storm at sea. He gave evil spirits orders they dared not disobey. He had actually raised the dead to life.

All this Judas, astute observer, had noted carefully. He had pondered it over in silence and secrecy and had told himself it was the chance of a lifetime. What might not he get out of it! To what heights of fame and power might he not hope to rise in the new kingdom, if only he could manage to ingratiate himself and win the notice and favor of Jesus! So he was vastly pleased and flattered on that morning three years ago when Christ had chosen himself and eleven others to be his close associates. The scene was still vivid in his mind; indeed he could never forget it. The previous evening Jesus had spent in prayer, kneeling throughout the night on the slope of the hill, and rising to his feet at the break of day.

He walks down. Already, very early though it still is, there are thousands waiting for him, some on the slope of the hill, and many more who have spilled over into the adjoining fields. Further evidence of the power of Christ, and it does not escape the eagle eye of Judas.

Jesus remains standing on the brow of the hill, a little elevated above the crowd, unhurried. He is going to select twelve men out of those around him, to be his constant companions, who will help him found and spread his kingdom. He looks over toward the right, he looks over to the left, he looks down the center and points out the precise man he wants in each case.

On that memorable morning those nearest to Christ heard the name Judas Iscariot, and it was passed from mouth to mouth till everyone present knew. If ever there was a genuine vocation this was it. They were like twelve novices or seminarians em-

barking on a campaign full of high promise, and calculated to satisfy the noblest aspirations to which any person could aspire.

The School of Christ

Christ wanted volunteers, not conscripts, because the motive is
love. He showed them the way, the ideal master of novices or
spiritual director, sure of what He wanted them to be and in-
structing them by word and example. Like most novices, they
had difficulties. They were raw enough material. Often they
fought shy of attempting to scale the heights of holiness to which
the Master pointed. But they had plenty of good will, and He had
much patience, realizing that before they attempted to run or
climb they should first learn to walk.

Little by little they found themselves accepting all that He
showed them. The novitiate lasted three years. By that time He
had won their hearts, and they were ready to die for Him. They
now saw life and its purpose in a new dimension, through His
eyes as you might say. It was reasonable and attractive; just what
their hearts were hungering for.

He drew all of them — with one exception. At the end of
three full years of novitiate under the guidance of a master who
was divine, Judas emerges a disillusioned man, soured, cynical,
thoroughly disappointed and even disgusted with the whole
project. Things had gone on tolerably well at first, but he began
by degrees to realize that he had made the biggest mistake of his
life on the morning he had accepted Christ's invitation to follow
him. This Jesus of Nazareth was a dreamer of dreams, an airy
visionary with no practical common sense. Judas had been glad
to link up with him for what he could get for himself in position
and hard cash. He sees now that he had it all wrong. Jesus had
gone around preaching with his head in the clouds.

Judas' first big shock came on the day when he stood listening to the sermon on the mount. He could hardly believe his

ears. Here was Jesus actually telling his audience to love poverty, to give their money away, to be glad when they were despised and delighted when suffering came their way. They should even pray for the very persons who made them suffer! Such incredible, insufferable nonsense! An emotional, sentimental idealist, talking to a mob of infatuated listeners who swallowed it all withot protest or grimace! A mighty kingdom to be sure would he raise up on these crazy principles. There was worse to come. All Christ's subsequent teaching followed the same pattern. There was, for instance, that ridiculous episode of the woman who poured out every drop (yes, that detail he had noted) of precious spikenard on the feet of Christ as he sat at table. Judas looked on narrowly with covetous eyes. He stormed inwardly at the sight of this waste and for once he could not let it pass without comment. What a shame, he expostulated, to throw away in this reckless manner what could have been sold for money, and that money given to the poor! But it was not the needs of the poor that were worrying Judas. St. John who was present, tells us with his customary candor: "Now he said this, not because he cared for the poor, but because he was a thief, and, having the purse, carried the things put into it" (John 12:6). Judas, in other words, used to help himself to the contributions.

What infuriated Judas most of all was that Jesus showed unmistakable approval of what this silly woman had done. Concentration on finance had blinded him to the primacy of the spiritual. He was convinced that the whole show was a farce and that the time had come for him to get out.

Growth of an Idea

Recently there had been a more serious development. Christ, utterly tactless, had the temerity to assail with merciless invective the pharisees and scribes, the men who had power and influence in high places. Admittedly they were no angels, but there is such a thing as the economy of truth, and Jesus, it would seem, had never heard of it. He tore the masks off the faces of these men and exposed them for just what they were. And this in front of the commoners, who of course knew all about it already but never dared mention it except in a whisper and between themselves. They were jubilant to find a man with the courage to speak out. The big people were furious and decided that Christ must be got out of the way.

Yes, Judas is embittered. He sees there is nothing for him to get from this harebrained scheme. But mere avarice does not account for his downfall.

Certainly he was interested in money. He liked the feel of it in his hands, and he joined up with Christ in the hope of getting more. He was pleased that Christ had appointed him bursar. Jesus had a least sufficient good sense to recognize his business capacity. This augured well for the future of Judas.

The administration of money, even in large sums, does not necessarily lead to spiritual shipwreck. There are many canonized kings and queens who used money correctly. What brought about disaster in the case of Judas was that his concentration on money ultimately despiritualized him. So the unworldliness of the whole campaign sickened him. He began to feel the otherworldly atmosphere pervading the community stuffy at first and then barely tolerable. He was ill at ease in the company of the brethren, and conversation with them was strained. He and they seemed to be living in two different worlds. Yes. It was time he got out. After three wasted years! But how?

He got an idea, began to turn it over vaguely in his mind and thought it might be the answer. At first it seemed outrageous, but by degrees he managed to live with it. He found himself thinking out ways and means. The facts were that Judas was short of money; that there was no money in the organization he had joined, and never likely to be; that, therefore, he was a misfit; that he would never have got himself into this awkward corner had he understood from the start what it implied; that, finally, Jesus was an embarrassment to the city potentates and it was clear they wanted to be rid of him.

No doubt, now if they could find an accomplice willing to hand him over, they would pay him well. This looked like an opportunity waiting for Judas. A swift and skillful move might save him still — perhaps. If he was to make that move and carry it off satisfactorily, it might well prove to be his first, if belated, step to real greatness. But conscience? Well, what of conscience? Judas had sense enough to realize that there are times when a man must take strong action and not worry about petty scruples. By this line of specious reasoning he was conditioned, or rather had conditioned himself. The suggestion no longer inspired horror. He had lulled his conscience into an uneasy slumber. The problem now was what practical steps to take. As a result of his ruminations within himself he had discovered a new drug that looked as if it could calm his restless mind. It now seemed to him, or at least he did his best to make it so seem, that to hand over Christ in the manner he was contemplating would, in fact, be an act of virtue. It was a duty he owed to his ecclesiastical superiors. Had they not issued an order requiring anybody who possessed information about the movements of Jesus of Nazareth to make it known at once to the authorities?

How much of Judas there is in all of us! We are adept at excusing ourselves, deceiving ourselves, stopping our ears and shutting our eyes, lest we see and hear what God wants us to do, our self-will pulling in the opposite direction.

The Climax

Disaster by this time is almost inevitable for Judas. That night, under cover of darkness, the wretched man slips down the street and knocks at the door of the high priest's house. Annas and his companions are seated inside discussing the interminable question, how to silence this irrepressible Jesus of Nazareth. They are frankly astonished to see Judas, a known disciple of the man they hate. What can he want with them, and at such an hour? He has no time for apologies or introductions. He has been driven in here by an unquiet hankering for something, anything almost, other than Jesus of Nazareth. "What will you give me," he blurts out, "if I will deliver him?"

Is there any mistaking his meaning? They observe him shrewdly. The lips twitching with nervous excitement and the eyes glowing with greed reassure them. In such a place and at such a time, "him" can mean no one but Jesus. He dare not pronounce the name. It sticks in his throat. By this time, we remember, "Satan had entered into him."

"What will you give me?" So he wants money. What would he say to thirty pieces of silver (the sum, as presumably he knew, that had to be paid to a master if his slave was injured)? Judas, dazzled by the glitter of the silver coins shining under the glare of the lighted lanterns, sweeps them into his wallet, seizes the quill pen and signs the contract by which he has bound himself to hand Christ over to them. "From that time he sought opportunity to betray him in the absence of the multitude" (Matthew 26:15). This is the horrible secret mentioned a few pages back of eating into the traitor's heart during the last supper. All arrangements have been completed, and this is the night when the deed is to be done. Christ, having failed to turn Judas back from his evil purpose, tries to protect at least his reputation. He told him: "What you have to do, do quickly." This did not compromise him before the others. They had no notion as to what lay concealed behind the simple commission. They scarcely adverted to it. Christ often gave such instructions to Judas to be carried out in his capacity as bursar.

So Judas goes out. "It was night," says St. John, a perfect description of the darkness descended on the soul of the traitor. This is the final break. He tells himself how good it feels to be emancipated forever from Christ and his collection of dreamers and find himself on the threshold of a new existence where he will be dealing with real men. No more realms "not of this earth"!

But he can scarcely have succeeded in blotting out from his memory the terrible words he had heard Christ say at the supper. "Yes, the Son of Man is going to his fate as the scriptures say he will, but alas for that man by whom the Son of Man is betrayed. Better for that man if he had never been born!" (Mark 14:21).

This "hard saying" of Christ does not necessarily mean that Judas was lost. The words were intended possibly to imply that the crime of Judas was so enormous in itself that it would be better for Judas not to be born rather than be guilty of it.

Did Judas succeed in filling the vacuum? The unfortunate man, his contract executed, rushes back madly to the enemies of Christ. He is carrying the thirty pieces of silver. They are burning his hands like coals of fire. "I have sinned," he shouts. "I have betrayed innocent blood." He flings the coins far from him, and they jingle as they fall on the marble floor. The spectators smile patronizingly. Judas has served them well. If he betrayed an innocent man, why, that is his own affair; it has nothing to do with them. Poor Judas, what had he lost and what had he gained?

He fled. In utter isolation he wandered out into the street. What to do, where to turn? If only he had found his way back to Christ! He walked as far as the valley of Hinnom, where there was a graveyard; he moved around in the midst of the tombs. It seemed he had no friend among the living. Why not seek friendship and companionship with the dead?

His body was found next morning, hanging from a tree. Judas died by his own hand because he could not rid himself of the conviction that his sin was too great to be forgiven.

Postscript

After I had finished writing about Judas I came upon the following quote from an enthralling book. It is called *Poustinia*, and the author is a Russian lady, Catherine de Hueck Doherty. "My father had a friend," she tells us, "whose name was Peter. He was well-born, of the nobility, the eldest son of an old Russian family. He was pretty close to what Americans would call a millionaire. He had much real estate and a lot of silver and gold in the bank.

"One day he came to my father and said: 'Theodore, I have been reading the gospels and I have decided, like so many before me, to accept them literally. I am going to collect my goods, especially my gold and silver. My farms, my real estate, I am giving to my family. The cash I own in the bank I shall change into gold and silver coins.' "

"He did so, and my father accompanied him throughout the whole transaction. He hired a huge dray, drawn by two horses. He filled it with several sacks, all of them containing gold and silver pieces. He then went, with my father, down into the slums of Petrograd, and there, house by house and family by family, he gave away all the money. When the sacks were empty he said: 'Now I have, in some measure, ransomed the thirty pieces of silver for which God was sold.' . . . "The last my father saw of him was just a silhouette against the setting sun — a man in a long white robe with a staff in his hand. He had no money in his bag nor a pocket in his gown. He had only some bread, water, salt, and his staff. Not even shoes. . . ." Like the little poor man of Assisi, reborn and living with us in the Seventies.

CAIAPHAS

"They led him away to Annas first." This man Annas had held the influential and lucrative position of high priest for several years, after which he was deposed by Pilate. His five sons each followed him in turn in the same position, and at the time of Our Lord's Passion the office had passed to Caiaphas, his son-in-law. This Caiaphas, notorious in the story of Christ, continued as high priest for no less than eighteen years, right through the period of the Pilate government. This, in itself, as we shall see presently, was no small achievement.

So it is clear that the Annas family was a powerful clique, a force to be reckoned with. They were the professedly religious people of the Jews, steeped deep in their knowledge of the law and fanatical in enforcing its observance in all its multitudinous and exasperating details. They have been aptly called "the Rothschilds of Palestine." Enormous perquisites flowed into their pockets from the revenues of the temple they controlled. Religion proved to be a sound investment. If they upheld it with such tenacity, their fervor and their zeal, ostensibly directed to the glory of God, never for a moment dimmed what it meant to them in hard cash for themselves.

The Arrest

The house of Annas and the house of Caiaphas were built on the same compound. You went in by a gate and you found the two dwellings inside, each facing the other, one on your right and one on your left. It was probably after midnight when the soldiers arrived with their prisoner, and old man Annas may have gone to

105

his bed. People might have been chary of disturbing him, but any annoyance he may have expressed was forgotten as soon as he heard the good news of the capture of the Nazarene.

"They led him away to Annas first." The Jews flattered Annas by still referring to him as high priest, though, once deposed, he had lost all claim to the title. He still wielded much influence in dictating policies binding on the people. Joseph Caiaphas, his son-in-law and the actual holder of the office, had to confess that he himself was no more than a tool in his hands. By submitting Christ to Annas for questioning and trial, Caiaphas was simply playing a part. This was a grave injustice since Annas, now out of office, had no right to sit in judgment or pronounce sentence on any man.

Jesus was brought along merely to provide entertainment for Annas. He looked curiously and appraisingly into the face of Christ, standing there in front of him with his hands tied. Annas walked laboredly over to a chair and seated himself, beaming with satisfaction. At last the hour had come for which he had so often wished. Nothing now remained except to trump up a case against Christ, bully Pilate into pronouncing sentence of death, then see to its execution and reduce this troublemaker to silence forever.

Meantime, by way of a little pleasant diversion, he would draw the man out and hear what he had to say for himself. How many followers did he have, Annas asked ingratiatingly, who were they, and what were some of the points he was propounding in this new doctrine of his? He knew the answers. He asked not for information but to give a semblance of formality to this illegal procedure.

Christ refused to be drawn. He treated the court with contempt. "I have spoken openly to the world," He reminded His questioner. "I have always taught in the synagogue and the temple where all the Jews resort. So why ask me? In secret I have spoken nothing. Ask those who heard me. They know what I said."

At this juncture a servant, standing close by and anxious to curry favor with his master, intervenes. With an extravagant showing of indignation and devotion to Annas, he addresses Christ. "How dare you use such language," he demands, "when addressing the high priest of God?" And the fellow lifts his hand and deals Jesus a heavy blow on the cheek, the first He has received in His Passion. (How many more would follow before it ended? And how many more ever since?)

This parody, designed to entertain Annas, drags on for possibly the best part of an hour. Meantime Caiaphas is busy in his own house on the other side of the compound. He must dispatch messengers all over the city, in every direction, to spread the good news. These are told to inform all the priests, ancients, and scribes that Jesus has been taken. Every member of the sanhedrin is alerted and told to proceed at once to the house of Caiaphas. Not a moment to lose. The job must be over and done with before the end of this very day. No need to mention His name. They begin to arrive posthaste. The whole place comes alive. A constant din of conversation. Everyone wants to know the details of the arrest. Each new arrival is greeted hurriedly and shown to his place in the council chamber. They seat themselves in two parallel rows, each facing the other, at the top a special chair reserved for the high priest.

Arrangements are all complete now. Only the presence of the accused man is wanting. These priests and elders have planned cold-blooded murder. They "assembled in the palace of the high priest, whose name was Caiaphas, and made plans to arrest Jesus by some trick and have him put to death" (Matthew 26:3). So far they have succeeded admirably. Show the man in. He is only a pawn in the game, but we cannot play it or win it without him. Word is sent across the compound to Annas, requesting him to permit Christ to come over. Annas has enjoyed himself and promises himself further amusement tomorrow. He rises, signals to the attendants to take Jesus away, and himself shuffles out of the room.

The Darkness Deepens

Every head of every member of the council turns towards the door when it opens to admit the prisoner — with hands bound all this time — and two soldiers with him as guards, one on the right and one on the left, till he reaches the place occupied by the high priest. There he stands, majestic, self-controlled, dignified in his hour of humiliation. This is the full Sanhedrin, judge and jury, seventy-two in all, though a few are probably missing. Their function is to administer impartial justice. Each man has been supplied with a quill pen and a sheet of parchment to make notes and take down the evidence. With this sickening, hypocritical setting all complete, the trial can now begin.

Suppose I find myself in some inconspicuous corner of that hall from which I can see and hear everything that is happening. Suppose, just before judge and jury have settled down to their task, that I emerge noiselessly, and tiptoe across the floor as far as the man who is sitting at the end of the row. I pluck him by the sleeve and ask him what exactly does he believe in his heart about this man, Jesus of Nazareth. Is he innocent or guilty, which does he think?

Surely a reasonable question to put to a responsible member of the jury. And what is the answer? Listen: "What a simpleton you are, my poor fellow! Do you imagine for a moment that we have the slightest interest in trying to decide whether he is guilty or not guilty? That has nothing to do with the case. No question could be more remote from our minds. What we have sworn to do is make quite certain that the man you see there standing before Caiaphas will be cold in death before the sun sets this evening. So please forget your baby-talk about innocence or guilt."

He guffaws, settles back comfortably into his armchair and proceeds to give his attention to what is going on.

This travesty of justice becomes the more galling and pronounced when we reflect on Caiaphas and his method of conducting the trial. He has set before himself the same precise aim as his colleagues. Jesus must die. Jesus must die today. Why? First of all because he claimed to be God. This they consider to be rank blasphemy, and they would be right if the claim were not supported by unanswerable arguments. These they refused to consider and evaluate. When Christ went to the lengths of raising a dead man to life, even then they hardened their hearts. In fact they refused even to examine the case and find out if the story was really true. They were not interested. Uncontrolled passion had blinded their reason. What did worry them was their own material prosperity and security. "Then the chief priests and pharisees called a meeting," writes St. John. 'Here is a man,' they said, 'working all these signs, and what action are we taking? If we let him go on in this way everyone will believe in him, and the Romans will come and destroy us and the holy places and the nation.' One of them, Caiaphas, the high priest of that year, said, 'You do not seem to have grasped the situation at all. You fail to see that it is better for one man to die for the people than for the whole nation to be destroyed' " (John 11:47).

He did not say this "of himself." He was inspired to say it inasmuch as he was high priest. His words had a far deeper significance than he realized. They meant that Jesus, "one man," should die, not only for the nation but for the whole world. "From that day," adds the apostle, "they were determined to kill him." Innocent or guilty, He must not be allowed to live. His death is first priority. What means are to be taken is beside the point. What charges, true or false, are brought up against Him is a matter of supreme indifference. One thing matters. One only. It matters enormously that Jesus of Nazareth be put out of the way.

He is a serious menace to the *status quo*. If he gets his way, what will become of the holy places, and, more specifically, what will become of the great temple, and, more specifically still, what will happen to the fat salaries of those who serve in it? Caiaphas will try to cloak over his real reasons for wanting the death of

Christ by whitewashing them with a veneer of piety and regard for religion. That he cared little for these in his heart is clear from the complete lack of interest he showed in the miracle of raising a dead man to life. A man abounding in worldly wisdom behaves like a fool. One man must die if Caiaphas is to hold his office of high priest and draw his salary. So "from that day they were determined to kill him."

Full Session

It speaks much for the tact and diplomacy of Caiaphas that during his sixteen years as high priest he never once crossed swords with the redoubtable Roman Governor Pontius Pilate. During all the troubles between Pilate and the people, the wily Caiaphas managed to steer an even keel and escape involvement in any debate. This cannot have been easy, for the governor was a difficult character who fell afoul of nearly everyone, including Herod. But Caiaphas was an exception. He maintained a semblance of friendship by consistently adopting a policy of subservience, and he found that Pilate liked it. From the first moments of the midnight trial of Christ Caiaphas realized that it was vitally important to keep up these relations. The claim of Jesus to be king might, he knew, infuriate the Roman. So Caiaphas must walk warily, avoiding any word or act which might seem to favor the pretender, "lest, perchance, there should be a tumult among the people."

He was aware that many of the populace believed in Christ and his fantastic notions. If these tried to make any sort of public demonstration, they must be ruthlessly crushed. Such scenes would antagonize Pilate, who was there to uphold the kingship of Caesar. What, then, he wanted to achieve was the death of Christ without involving himself in complications between Jews and Romans.

Given that picture, it will come as no surprise that Caiaphas and his colleagues had suborned "many false witnesses" to swear to the guilt of the accused man. They are lined up here at this midnight seance, eager to pour out the tales they have concocted, collect their money, and be away. But from the very start of the trial it looked as if the whole facade was about to collapse. The witnesses were not only false; they were utterly stupid, and their stupidity must be traced back to whoever had coached them.

First of all, the charges they had framed were puerile. They had to do with some statement attributed to Jesus, to the effect that He would destroy the great temple and rebuild it in three days. What possible interest could Pilate have in such a cock-and-bull story? He cared nothing for their temple, and he openly scorned the fanaticism that seemed to be part of their religion. A moment's reflection should have shown the fabricators of this piece of "evidence" that Pilate would never condemn a man for such absurdities. Equally ridiculous to waste time discussing whether Christ had broken the sabbath or not. To Pilate the sabbath meant nothing.

Caiaphas sat listening, inwardly seething with rage. But there were further egregious mistakes. It was bad enough that the stories invented were silly, but what added to the mismanagement was that not even on these obviously foolish charges did the witnesses agree. They contradicted one on other! The whole trial had evidently been prepared in advance, but the rehearsal reflected no credit on whoever directed it.

The astute Caiaphas thought quickly. The mastermind behind the trial was not to be outwitted. Until now Christ had not spoken a word. He must be forced to say something if the situation was to be saved. Whatever words he used might give the high priest a chance to cover up the mistakes and begin the trial all over again.

So he stood up and spoke to the prisoner. "Have you no answer to these charges?" he asked. "What answer have you to the charges these men have brought against you?" But Jesus held His peace. Speech would have been superfluous. He treated the court with contempt. Everyone in the hall would have admitted, if he dared, that the trial was a farce.

So Jesus spoke not a word. His silence shows a strength which to us is almost terrifying, so accustomed are we to acting very differently ourselves. We cannot bear to be shown up in a false light. Let somebody misquote us or misinterpret our words or actions, however unintentionally, and we rush to rectify the mistake. Even more forcefully do we defend ourselves if lies are told. Jesus, accused in half-truths, "held his peace."

"You Have Said It"

This persistent silence is maddening. It enrages Caiaphas. If this obstinate man cannot be made to say something, anything, it will be clearer than ever that his accusers are liars and hypocrites.

The high priest regards his victim with blazing eyes. "Have you no answer?" he shouts. Jesus returns the look, staring His tormentor full in the face and saying nothing. "Have you no answer?" This extraordinary question is tantamount to saying: "Accusations have been brought against you. No proof can be offered. The witnesses have shown that they invented charges they cannot substantiate. So it is now your turn to speak. Our evidence has fallen apart. Say something to compromise yourself and supply fresh matter for accusation." Caiaphas talks like a man demented. He is angered by the stupidity and bungling in the preparations for trial. It cannot be said that his own contribution did much, so far, to patch up the mistakes.

Still no answer. Still that tantalizing silence. Still Christ stands there seeming to read his soul with those piercing eyes of His. Caiaphas, on the verge of desperation, sees a sudden, unexpected flash of light. "Are you the Christ?" he asks. "I adjure you by the living God that you tell us if you are the Son of God."

This finally loosened the tongue of Christ. It brought an

immediate reply, for now Caiaphas is speaking in his official capacity as high priest, God's accredited representative, however unworthy and corrupt. The judge, fearful lest this last effort might fail, had prefaced it by a most solemn formula: "I adjure you by the living God. . . ."

Christ's answer? He told Caiaphas: "You say that I am the Son of God." He was employing a well-known hebraism here which was recognized as an emphatic affirmation. He had used it last night. He foretold that one of those sitting at table with Him would betray Him. When Judas asked: "Is it I, master?" he was told: "You have said it." Again later on, when Pilate put Him the question, "Are you the king of the Jews?" the reply was: "You say that I am."

So everyone in the hall where the trial is in progress understands that Christ, without any doubt, is claiming to be, in the most literal sense, the Son of God. Other holy men in the past had described themselves similarly, but it is clear that they spoke figuratively, whereas the expression used by Christ makes it quite clear that He is claiming to be divine, one with the Father and equal to Him in all things.

"You say I am the Son of God." Caiaphas is jubilant. At last, only in the nick of time, he has extracted from the lips of Jesus a statement such as he wanted. Jesus has committed Himself. He has "confessed," and there has been no brainwashing like that to which so many of His faithful followers have been subjected in our day.

But Jesus is not finished. "I tell you solemnly, Caiaphas," He goes on, "and warn you that you will see the Son of Man sitting at the right hand of the power of God and coming in the clouds of heaven." Today Caiaphas is judge and Jesus is the accused. In the final day the roles will be reversed. On that day Christ will demand from Caiaphas a strict account of the manner in which he has administered the authority vested in him. Most of us share in that authority, in greater or lesser degree, as parents, priests, teachers, employers, state officials. We dare not play with it according to our own selfish motives. We have to administer it according to the principles clearly laid down for us by God.

But Caiaphas, again perhaps like ourselves, turns a deaf ear to this warning. He concentrates, rather, on the "confession" of Christ. With a single stroke of his genius he has shifted the whole foundation of this trial from sinking sands and has set it on solid ground. He has swayed the entire assembly to enthusiastic acceptance of the new approach.

What was his own reaction? He began by taking hold of his tunic with both hands and in a dramatic gesture ripping it down the middle. A Jew commonly did this when he was deeply grieved or shocked. In the present context it was the contemptible smokescreen of a hypocrite. It was a pretense intended to deceive those who saw it into believing that the high priest's religious sense was outraged.

He tells the onlookers, in a stage whisper meant to convey his horror and alarm: "Jesus has blasphemed." The punishment for blasphemy is death, so the prisoner must die. Witnesses can now be dispensed with. We know the truth. We have heard it ourselves. What did they think should be done? The verdict is unanimous. Let Jesus of Nazareth die! Caiaphas' great moment. Tearing his garments seems outwardly to express sorrow and shock; actually it conceals his intense delight.

All That Night

A disgusting orgy follows. "Then did some spit in his face and buffet him. Others struck his face with the palms of their hands. They jeered him and hit him. They blindfolded him, struck him and called on him to prophesy who it was that struck him. And blaspheming, many other things they said against him" (Cf. Matt. 26:67).

Is there any gesture more expressive of utter contempt than to spit deliberately into a person's face? And why did they blindfold Him? Was it because they could not bear the limpid purity shining in those eyes and reproaching them for their degrading behavior?

When the midnight revel in his house at last broke up Caiaphas dismissed his companions. But not until he had warned them in the most emphatic way that every one of them was to report unfailingly at Pilate's palace soon after dawn. Let them go home now and snatch an hour or two of sleep and then proceed at once to the place assigned. They are urged; they are threatened too; Annas and Caiaphas will know how to deal with defaulters.

What about the Nazarene? "He remained in bonds all that night," writes St. Ignatius — from the time of His arrest and right up to the present moment, and bound He would remain till His hands were freed to enable Him to carry His cross. For the rest of this night the soldiers have *carte blanche* to do with Him just exactly as they please. There is only one limitation. In stern language they are warned of the price they will have to pay should Jesus escape from their hands. This He has been known to do on previous occasions. Let it happen now at their peril! So, well satisfied that they have done a fine night's work, priests and ancients adjourn and retire to their respective homes.

There is no evidence of sorrow or remorse in what is known of the subsequent history of Joseph Caiaphas. After the death of Christ he continued on his career of hatred, as is instanced by his treatment of John and Peter, disciples of Jesus. These had been preaching Christ with much success, and to prove their credentials they had worked a first-class miracle. They would pay for their indiscretion. The two were scourged and imprisoned, and they would certainly have forfeited their lives, only that their persecutors feared that a revolt among the people might follow. Caiaphas, tactful and sagacious as ever, would keep out of trouble. As for Peter and John, "they came forth from the council chamber, rejoicing that they counted worthy to suffer for the name of Jesus."

Caiaphas shows up in an equally unfavorable light when he makes himself an accomplice in stoning St. Stephen to death. His implacable hatred of Christ can be seen in the commission he gave to Saul, fanatic and bigot. After Calvary Caiaphas continued his policy of subservience to Rome. For sixteen years he reveled in the possession of wealth and power. He was then deposed and humiliated. What the offense was is not known. Having occupied the center of the stage so long, he now moved into the wings.

The curtain dropped, and he was forgotten. Perhaps in his hour of disgrace he recognized his folly, his foolish vanity. Maybe he repented. It was not till the prodigal son had sunk to the level of the pigsty and the swine that he realized what was the only correct course to take: "I will arise and go back to my father."

PILATE

Some people said that Christ was the Son of God; others that He was a liar and a hypocrite. Some people were favorably impressed by His miracles; others, who could not deny the facts, attributed to the devil the power Christ was using. Some said that never did man speak as He spoke; others said He was mad, and they wondered how any sensible person could listen to Him. Some said He had done all things well; others that He was a criminal and a malefactor. On Good Friday the crowd demanded that He be crucified, although many of them had probably acclaimed Him king on the preceding Sunday. He went into the synagogue, and all who heard Him "were astonished by the gracious words that came from his lips." Yet, before He had finished speaking, these same people were "enraged, and they hustled him out of the town . . . intending to throw him down the cliff" (cf. Luke 4:16 ff.).

All of which goes to show how foolish it is to be unduly swayed by men's opinions. "It makes not the slightest difference to me," St. Paul tells the Corinthians, "whether you, or any other human tribunal, find me worthy or not. . . . The Lord alone is my judge" (1 Corinthians 4:3-4).

For want of a healthy independence of what men will say and think about us, we act too often against our conscience. This is precisely what happened to Pilate when he had to make the most momentous decision of his whole life. He had to choose between Christ and Caesar. He was convinced of the innocence of Christ. Therefore, he had only one lawful course — to dismiss the case at once. But, as a creature of the mighty Caesar, he must play for safety. He hedged and hesitated and compromised and ended up by condemning Christ to death. Had he done otherwise, he would have been reported to Rome, and it would be a black mark against him to have seemed to condone the pretensions of Christ to be king of the Jews.

Beware

He hated these Jews and was heartily hated by them in turn. He knew they had power to injure or even ruin his reputation with the emperor. If they succeeded he might be deposed and never be able to regain his position. Caution and tact were all the more necessary because Pilate had made two bad blunders already. Soon after his appointment he had embarked on a scheme intended to demonstrate his loyalty to the emperor and win his favor. He sent his men bearing images of Caesar to the temple, with instructions that these were to be set up in the holy place. The people went frantic at what seemed to them a sacrilege. For a whole week they demonstrated in front of Pilate's house, refusing to go away till he ordered the odious statues to be removed. They would not take no for an answer; they would die first.

Pilate had to yield, and the commotion died down. But only for a while. To teach the Jews who was master, Pilate ordered a number of shields, suitably inscribed, to be hung on the walls of Herod's house. Another outbreak of fury, but this time the people ignored Pilate and sent their complaint direct to the emperor himself. The answer came back that the shields were to be removed at once. Pilate was severely reprimanded and told that in future he must respect the religious feelings of the Jews.

Emboldened by their double victory and gloating over the humiliation of the governor, the mob was all the more menacing when the time came to extract from Pilate the death sentence against Christ. As we shall see, "he feared the people."

His second big mistake had to do with the spending of public money. There was a shortage of water in the city, and he built an aquaduct, forty-seven miles long, which carried vast supplies through a system of tunnels and windings, filling the huge cisterns underneath the floor of the temple. All went well till Pilate announced that the cost of this operation should be met by money taken from the funds of the temple treasury. This started up another storm. Pilate had not foreseen any opposition but the religious sense of the citizens was again outraged. Pilate scattered several of his men among them, disguised as civilians, and ordered them to beat up the crowds and disperse them by force. They exceeded their orders, and many of the rioters were killed.

These complications serve to throw light on the mentality of Pilate during the trial of Jesus. They influenced him in coming to his fatal decision. He must not take any more risks with Caesar. No more damaging stories must be allowed to reach his ears.

Conscience

We find four distinct warnings given to Pilate in the course of the trial of Christ. The first of these came from Jesus Himself. If Pilate, before meeting Him, was under the impression that he was being called upon to deal with some Eastern fanatic making some preposterous claims to divinity, he was disabused after a very few minutes in the presence of Christ. This man was no felon or adventurer. There was the tranquillity and majestic dignity with which he bore himself, in sharp contrast to the rowdiness of his accusers. There was his astonishing self-possession, while the mob all around him hissed and yelled in a paroxysm of uncontrolled rage. The personality of Christ made a favorable impression on His judge from the start. The words spoken by the prisoner were the second warning to Pilate.

There is calm and restraint in his utterances. There is profound wisdom and material for serious reflection in what he has to say, leagues removed from anything remotely resembling the incoherence and jabberings of a madman. Pilate is overawed; he is puzzled; he assures himself he will never commit such a person as the Nazarene. Christ declined to speak a single word to the incestuous Herod. But he talks to Pilate, answering his questions, questioning Pilate himself, giving him points to help him in adjudicating the case, looking at him not in anger but in sorrow.

Pilate had been summoned from his bed at this unearthly hour. He arrived, irritated at the disturbance, yawning and prepared to deal with the Galilean summarily, with the contempt and rudeness which no doubt was all he expected and deserved. But on coming face to face with Christ, all Pilate's defenses fell. Never before had he met such a man. There was that intangible entity we call personality, which in this case attracted him powerfully. This, and the words of Christ, were the two first warnings, or, if you like, the two first graces, offered to the sorely-harrassed Pontius Pilate.

Next there came that mysterious message from his wife Claudia. "Have nothing to do with that just man," she wrote, "for I have suffered many things this day in a dream because of him."

Pilate, already bewildered by his contact with Christ, is now pulled up once more by this third appeal to his conscience. What can Claudia mean? Clearly she was convinced that it was something important and urgent. Her husband should know about it immediately and not fail to act upon it. Herod had lulled his conscience to sleep, but Pilate was still sensitive to its warnings.

The fourth and final stirring to his conscience came from an unexpected quarter. We remember that at one stage (about which we shall be speaking soon again) the judge sent the prisoner to Herod. Herod would have nothing to do with the case and returned Christ to Pilate. Once more they stand on the balcony face to face, Christ and this sorely-perplexed judge in whose soul a battle is raging, between what is right and what is wrong. "From henceforth," St. John tells us, "Pilate sought to release him." With this in view he had recourse to different subterfuges.

They all failed, ignominiously, one after the other. The mob, goaded on by priests and ancients, understood that the moment has struck to play their trump card. The death sentence must be extorted from Pilate, now or never.

"If you let this man go," they shouted up at him, "you are no friend of Caesar. For whoever makes himself a king speaks against Caesar. . . . This man ought to die because he made himself the Son of God." "When Pilate heard that, he feared the more." "Friend of Caesar . . . Son of God. . . ." He wanted to keep on good terms with Caesar, but the phrase "Son of God" smote his conscience.

The warning, his last one, came through unmistakably clear. He was superstitious, a religious person after a fashion. For the general run of Jews and their observances and beliefs he had nothing but contempt. But *this* Jew was different. There was something unearthly about him. "He made himself the Son of God!"

They were determined to press the advantage they saw they had gained. Pilate, finding the agony of suspense no longer bearable, longing to be finished with this whole tormenting business, gave in at last, throwing Jesus to them, as we might say, and telling them to take him out of his sight and crucify him. An innocent lamb delivered over the fury of the bloodthirsty wolves!

Four warnings resulting in this deplorable anticlimax. Pilate dallied and compromised when he should have taken a firm grip of the situation from the start. He felt himself compelled now, at this stage, to do a deed his soul loathed. We may not let ourselves be too hard on him, for, Pilate-like, we have stifled the voice of conscience many a time. How many warnings and promptings and actual graces and lights from the Holy Spirit and stirrings of divine love have we experienced over the years? To what bright holiness might we not have attained by now had we been more faithful in corresponding with these divine communications? But Christ's power to sanctify is not limited by circumstances of time or place. "It is well worthwhile striving to become a saint, even if you were assured you had only a quarter of an hour to live" (St. Francis de Sales).

Compromise

There is a series of warnings in the story of Pilate. There is also a catalogue of compromises. On his first meeting with the Jews, early on Good Friday morning, they made their position perfectly clear. What they were determined to have was the death sentence against Christ. Let Pilate pronounce it and be finished with it, for they would take nothing else. Why drag him into this brawl? the governor wanted to know. Why not judge the man according to their own laws and leave Pilate out? Why? "Because," they answered, "it is not lawful for us to put any man to death." So their purpose is stated without ambiguity. They know what they want. The next move is Pilate's. He will spare trouble all round if he dispatches this business immediately.

He looked down on them from his place on the balcony. He hated them. He despised them. They knew it, and he wanted them to know. But he had to confess that he feared them too. Their determined, menacing faces showed him that, in their present hostile mood, they were capable of turning the whole city and countryside into a shambles.

He parried. Why, he asked, did they want this man put to death? "If he were not an evildoer," they answered sulkily, "we would not have delivered him up to you." "But the specific charge," the governor insisted, "what is it?" "We have found him," they said, "perverting the nation, forbidding to give tribute to Caesar and saying he is Christ the king."

Pilate left the balcony and summoned the prisoner to follow him into a private room. Jesus admitted he was a king. "But my kingdom is not of this world. If it were, my servants would certainly strive that I should not be delivered into the hands of the Jews. ... Everyone who is of the truth hears my voice."

"Truth?" echoed Pilate. "What is truth?" And he went back to the balcony and the impatient crowd without waiting for an answer. "I can find no reason for putting this man to death," he reported to them. They felt they were losing ground. They became defiant. "He is sowing revolution among the people," they told him. "He began up in Galilee, and he has been filling the whole country, from there to here, with his doctrine."

The governor sees a way out, his first compromise. "Galilee?" he repeats. "Does Jesus, then, come from Galilee? Right. In that case take him to Herod, tetrarch of Galilee, and let him handle the case just as he sees fit himself." They are disappointed and furious, but they have no option. Pilate heaves a sigh of relief. This stroke of genius soothes his conscience. He has shuffled off all responsibility. Perhaps, as the mob disperses, he retires to his private room and starts to write an account of the affair to Tiberius. Nor would he have failed to underline his own skill and tact in handling the affair.

Before signing and sending off his report he rereads it and grins with satisfaction. This will help to reinstate Pilate in the good graces of his all-powerful master. But his pleasant reverie receives a jolt. To his horror and disgust he hears the crowd shouting and realizes that he has them on his hands still. They are back, and Jesus is with them. Just when he believed he had shaken himself free of a most distasteful task, here they are again.

The return of Jesus and the increased anger of his enemies at this delay in having sentence passed marks the failure of Pilate's first compromise. He is now driven to try another, and this second compromise points up to a man who would seem to be on the verge of losing his reason. He summons the priests and magistrates to a private conference. "This man is innocent," he tells them. "Neither Herod nor I can find any crime in him for which he should die. I will chastise him, *therefore*, and let him go." Was a more illogical "therefore" ever written or spoken? But why worry? The sentence concerns only Jesus, and He does not matter! Anything is good enough for Him! He is the reject of everyone. Nobody wants Him. Judas does not want Him, so he sells Him to the priests. Caiaphas does not want Him, so he hands Him over to Pilate. Pilate tries to get rid of Him by passing Him on to Herod. Herod dresses Him up as a public clown, parades Him along the street and lands Him back on Pilate once more. Christ, a pawn in their game!

The great rejection! "Hear O ye heavens and give ear, O earth, for the Lord has spoken. I have brought up children and have exalted them, but they have despised me" (Isaiah 1:2). Our world today might fairly be compared to a great lunatic asylum; or to a vast jungle, where men prowl about, hating one another, ignoring each other's fundamental rights, treating one another with a cruelty compared with which the brutality of the wild beasts is almost leniency. Why has this happened? What has gone wrong? The great rejection is with us still. Christ is the way, but we have gone astray. Christ is the truth, but with Pilate, we ask contemptuously what truth is; we do not wait for the answer; we prefer lies; truth will never permit one to get on in this crooked world. Christ is the life, but we prefer death — death to the soul by sin and death to the body by wholesale slaughter. Christ is the light of the world, but "men loved darkness rather than the light, because their works were evil" (John 3:19).

All this, we feel confident, does not apply to the readers of a book like this. For them, who sincerely try to know and love and follow Christ, the sheer truth of the lostness of Christ, which is the basic ailment of our world, will be a challenge to make reparation and unite in a crusade to *bring Christ back.*

The Second Compromise

"I will chastise him, therefore, and let him go." The evangelists merely state that Jesus was scourged. They give no details. The scene was so revolting that they seem incapable of putting a description of it on paper. Here is what they tell us: "Then Pilate took Jesus and scourged him. . . . They led him away into a court of the palace, and they called together to him the whole band. Stripping him, they put a scarlet cloak about him. And plaiting a crown of thorns, they put it on his head, and a reed in his right hand. They came to him, and, bowing the knee before him, they mocked him. They began to salute him, saying: 'Hail, king of the Jews.' "

"They struck him with the palms of their hands. And spitting upon him, they took the reed and smote him with it on the head. . . ." I suppose there is no expression of contempt more degrading than deliberately to spit into a person's face. They spat into the face of Christ, and the spittle remained congealed on his beard till the end, because he was powerless to do anything to remove it.

Pilate asked: "What is truth?" On an earlier page of this book we insisted that the Passion is no mere invention which comes out of the writer's imagination. It *is* the truth. We kneel here at the scourging of Christ, to look and meditate and pray. If this one harrowing scene alone were to grip us it would set our feet on the road to holiness as nothing else. The mob could hear the strokes, for the garrison yard was quite near. We can hear them too, for today Christ is being scourged in the members of His mystical body.

The echo of these strokes reverberates in the story of that giant of God, Jozsef Cardinal Mindszenty. Listen. "The major brought me back to the cell. It was about three o'clock in the morning. Two guards pushed the table away from the middle of the room. The major shouted to me to undress. I did not obey. He beckoned to his assistants. Together with them he pulled off my clown's jacket and trousers. Then they went out and searched furiously around the corridor. Suddenly a massively-built lieutenant appeared. 'I was a partisan,' he said. His language was Hungarian but not his savage, hate-filled face. I turned away. He drew back but suddenly came charging at me, kicking me with all his might.

"Both of us fell against the wall. Laughing diabolically he exclaimed: 'This is the happiest moment of my life.' The words were unnecessary. I could read his feelings in the distorted, sadistic features.

"The major produced a rubber truncheon and began beating me, first on the soles of my feet and then raining blows on my whole body. In the corridor and adjacent rooms raucous laughing of sadistic delight accompanied the blows. The men and women who had been at the interrogation were, apparently, near. . . . The major was soon breathing heavily but he did not slacken his blows. In spite of his exertions the beating obviously gave him intense pleasure.

"I clenched my teeth but did not succeed in remaining wholly mute. And so I whispered softly from pain. Then I was dressed and taken back to interrogation. Once more my signature was demanded. I refused it again, saying: 'This is not my confession.' Once more I was beaten. For the third time they demanded my signature — without success. For the third time they tried to thrash it out of me with the rubber truncheon, wielded with undiminished force, to the accompaniment of howls of laughter from the spectators. Then again they ordered me to sign and again I replied: 'As soon as I am shown a record which contains only what I said, what I said and nothing more or less, then I will do what you ask.' They replied with the same tiresome formula: 'Here it is the police who decided what is confessed, not the defendant.' "

The similarity between this scene and the scourging and mockery of Our Lord is so striking as to be almost frightening. This becomes clearer according as we take the two episodes and compare them in detail.

There are points of contrast also. Pilate was a weak character who would not face up to an issue and would try to shuffle off responsibility from his own shoulders onto the shoulders of somebody else. But in this invincible cardinal God has given to His Church another St. Paul, "a lonely but truly determined man, a great freedom-fighter, who refused, time and time again to let political expediency supersede the principles in which he believed and the faith by which he stood." Here is a typical sentence from his pen: "I am convinced that even the greatest personal sacrifice shrinks to insignificance when the cause of God and the Church are at stake."

Ecce Homo

Pilate brings forth his victim, crowned with thorns and clothed in tattered purple in mockery of His kingship. It is very likely that Christ needed support in order to be able to stand. He is a little elevated above the crowds, and the judge points Him out to them with the words: "Behold the Man." Surely their hatred will now at last be satisfied; surely He has suffered enough for the crime of being an innocent man. But he has underestimated the depth of their frenzy and fury. Goaded by their leaders, they cry out: "Away with him; crucify him." "But why?" asks Pilate, "What evil has he done?" They ignore his question. They have outwitted him. They have him in their hands now, and it is no longer necessary to frame a charge against the prisoner. "They cried out the more: 'Crucify him.'"

"Shall I crucify your king?" and there was a note of unmistakable scorn in the tone in which Pilate put the question.

"We have no king but Caesar." Even the hated Roman is preferred before Christ. The second compromise, like the first, has proved itself a dismal failure. The situation is more complex than ever. Almost in despair, Pilate is on the point of yielding. But he suddenly stops short and is silent. Another idea has just crossed his mind. It will mean further compromise, but there is a chance that it may yet save the life of a just man.

There was always a big influx of visitors to Jerusalem at this time of the year, drawn by the passover celebrations. The occasion was honored by the liberating of any one prisoner whom the people would choose. Would there be any chance that the visitors would ask for Christ to be set free? If their demand was forceful enough and loud enough it might contradict and even overrule those crying out for His crucifixion. At any rate he would make the attempt.

It happened that there was a notorious villain in jail at the time. His name was Barabbas. He was accused on at least two counts, against the authority of both Jews and Romans. So both parties wanted him out of the way. It was not to be thought of that anyone would wish this fellow to be at large again. Pilate sends for Barabbas and orders him to stand beside Christ. They stood in an enclosed space, which St. John calls "the pavement." Its area is about 3,000 square yards. It has been identified in our own day. The floor consists of several immense flagstones, on some of which it is still possible to trace the designs according to which the soldiers played their games of chance.

Here, then, is the spot on which the two men stood on that first Good Friday morning. The Jews were some distance off, under the archway. They would consider themselves defiled if they went into the hall. A supreme example of straining out a gnat and swallowing a camel? So Pilate went out to them, and pointing to Christ and Barabbas, he said: "You have a custom that I should release to you one prisoner on this occasion. Which of these two do you wish to go free — Barabbas, whose record of crime you know very well, or Jesus of Nazareth in whom no crime can be found?"

This is the final challenge, and the priests and ancients must see to it that the response is immediate and imperious. "Give us Barabbas!" they shout back, and with violent gesticulations they urge the mob to take up the cry. They are only too successful.

"Give us Barabbas!"

"And," says Pilate, insistently, "what am I to do with Jesus of Nazareth?" A senseless question: seeing that it was put by a judge regarding a man he had declared to be innocent, you would say Pilate must have lost his reason. He finally capitulates.

All his compromises have collapsed. If only he had been man enough to take the situation firmly in hand from the beginning! Now he is morally forced to do what his soul loathes.

"Take him, you," he tells them, "and crucify him, for I find no cause in him." And the fearful answer: "His blood be upon us and upon our children!"

Pilate strides across the pavement, sits down in the place of judgment, signals to a slave to fetch him a basin of water. The slave leaves and returns and kneels before his lord, holding the bowl in both hands. Pilate dips his hands deep, stands up and walks over to the edge of the balcony. Holding out his hands, still dripping, he cries: "I am innocent of the blood of this just man." We have much sympathy with Pilate, but we have to say that all the waters in the Jordan and Tiber cannot wash the blood of Christ off his hands.

Afterwards

It is comforting to remember what tradition has to tell us about Pilate's subsequent career. He fell from power, was sent into exile and got the grace to become a Christian. The Abyssinian Church lists his name among the saints and keeps his feast on June 25. There is a high pyramid on the banks of the Rhone that is said to be his burial place. Tertullian writes that in spite of his weakness, he was a Christian "in the fugitive, impotent longings of his soul." The tradition that his wife Claudia Procula became a Christian dates from the second century. Legends have grown up around Pilate. Scholars view many of them with extreme caution. Hatred brought about the death of Christ. He is hated still. I once stood in Hyde Park, London, close to two men who had given up the practice of the faith. They kept on heckling and interrupting the priest who was addressing the crowd. That is common enough. But what rankles in my mind to this day is the glint of hatred in their eyes and in their distorted faces. I imagine that if they had dared they would have dragged the priest down, beaten him, possibly killed him.

We live in a world of hatred, and that is why the Passion is relevant today. We have to bring Christ back. He is invincible. He has overcome the world. He won the victory on Calvary.

HEROD

The trial of Jesus Christ before Herod Antipas has rightly been described as the most humiliating scene in the entire Passion. The truth of this will emerge, we suggest, from a threefold consideration — the judge, the prisoner, and the sentence. Such a judge! Such a prisoner! Such a sentence!

The Judge

Herod was a man who served one god, only one. That god's name was pleasure, and he had only one commandment: "I am the lord your god; you shall not have strange gods before me." Herod was the willing slave of pleasure — not the pleasure of the scholar who finds delight in his books and tolerates with difficulty any intrusion on his studies; still less the pleasure and delight of the person who has lost his heart to Christ and longs to share his love for him with the whole world. No. Herod, like St. Paul, had learned early enough in life the existence of a law in his members fighting against the law of his mind. But differently from the apostle, he had come to terms with this opposition. He called a truce with the law of the flesh and began to worship it. It became more and more demanding. It was proving itself to be insatiable. And "whoever commits sin is *the slave of sin*" (John 8:34). Before this idol he knelt, even prostrated himself in adoration. "Man, when he was in honor, did not understand; he is compared to the brute beasts and becomes as one of them" (Psalm 49 [48]:13). Christ's other two judges, Caiaphas and Pilate, were no angels, but in comparison with Herod, they might be regarded as almost ascetics.

Herod never knew the meaning of true love, only the deceptive, frustrating counterfeit. His father had become a veritable savage, a ruthless tyrant, dreaded and hated and shunned by everybody.

Herod I had the blood of the innocent babies on his hands, but it washed off and was forgotten, as easily then as it is today, in our modern, efficient slaughterhouses. In these millions are murdered — two such crimes every minute, according to Archbishop Fulton Sheen. We do not like to hurt people's feelings by giving the operation a harsh name. Murder? No. It is kinder and shows more consideration for our sensitivity to talk about the termination of an unwanted pregnancy.

Herod the Great, father of the man who judged Christ, ruled his house with a rod of iron, crushing his son into a way of life where he had to learn that nothing was expected from him but unqestioning subservience. Father and son hated each other heartily and did nothing to hide their feelings. The younger man squirmed under the lash of his father's fierce invective. It was with difficulty that he restrained himself from retaliating even with physical violence.

The old man died of a foul disease, having reigned as virtual king of Palestine for over thirty years. No tears were shed at his funeral that day. His son stood with the rest of the crowd, looking on at the proceedings, stolid, passive and dry-eyed, while the body was lowered into the grave. This was the day of his liberation. He had waited thirty years for it. There was nothing now to prevent his plunging headlong into an existence free of all restraint. The prospect was thrilling.

Now life would begin. He succeeded his father as tetrarch of Galilee and, like him, held the position for nearly thirty years. He was a puppet king, little more than a figurehead, with plenty of time on his hands. The Romans who appointed him were not concerned at all to control what he did or left undone, provided only that where their methods of governing were concerned he was satisfied to lie low and not interfere.

Nothing could have pleased the young man better. This aimless existence, free of all responsibility, gave him ample opportunity to enjoy himself. He had every intention of doing so. He began by setting up a sumptuous villa at Machaerus, a table-land overlooking the Red Sea, high up in the hills. He had a good salary, an easy job and security. What more could anybody want? Flatterers and parasites flocked to the place by the score, coming and going by night and by day. They willingly paid him lip-service, encouraging him in his flippant living, filled with fun and laughter. Lady friends were available at three a penny. This was Utopia, the dawning of a new life, breaking in on the darkness and slavery and terror endured under his father, now happily defunct and asleep in his grave.

No one had to tell him how to compensate himself. He flung restraint and decency and convention to the winds. Passion tightened its grip on him every day, goading him to further excesses. Each such excess, when it had been indulged in, left him with a larger void in his heart; each persisted in promising complete satisfaction if yielded to once more, and the infatuated victim allowed himself to go on being deceived.

According as his hopes remained unfullfilled, he began, as the years moved on, to develop a fierce temper. He became more callous and more cruel, more gross and repulsive to look upon. There were some fearful bouts of quarrelling and wrangling. He had to be petted and coaxed and humored like a spoiled child till he was induced to smile again. He would then forget his annoyance — till the next time. He never grew up. At thirty he was immature still.

Red Light

Herod's brother Philip, tetrarch of a neighboring district, seems by contrast to have been of a more even and retiring disposition. He had married Herodias, and they had one child, a girl named Salome. They were an ill-matched couple from the beginning, incompatibility of temperament often leading to abuse and squabbling. Salome, growing up in this atmosphere, had little of the joys of childhood. She became precocious beyond her years. Listening to the coarse language between her father and mother, she became abnormally curious to find out what was implied in their accusations and insinuations. She was mentally unhealthy in her childhood, so the later developments in her character need not surprise us.

Philip was a stay-at-home, something of a recluse. He liked the quiet life, "the tranquillity of order," when the atmosphere of the house permitted it — during the not-infrequent absences of his wife and daughter. In our day he would have been happy to sit watching television or reading a paper and enjoying his pipe. Herodias was restless, a gadabout, liking to shine in society. She was pleased to hear herself talking and flattered when men listened and joked and admired. Daring suggestions she received with a pretense of being shocked; inwardly she gloried in the power she felt she had to attract and fascinate her men friends. She enjoyed parties, drank freely, danced lithely, tried her best not to look her age, laughed and smiled charmingly — vicacious, witty, adventuresome. If her conduct did not always measure up to the standards expected by anchoritic Philip, that was just too bad.

Herod loved nothing more than lavish festivities, with tables groaning and wine freely flowing, with any number of the right type of guests, sparkling conversation seasonably spiced, and the lot interspersed with song and dance and music, night turned into day.

To one of these celebrations came Herodias and Salome. They were welcomed warmly by their host, who was waiting for them in the brilliantly lighted hall. They had a marvelous evening. The lady enjoyed herself immensely. She congratulated Herod on the splendid turnout as she was leaving. He was very glad she and Salome had enjoyed themselves. But they must not be strangers. He would very much wish to have them again. She beamed delightedly and promised. The two of them, Herod and Herodias, had exercised an immediate, powerful attraction on each other. The red light was showing, but what did they care? They did not want to see it. It warned, but it gave a thrill too. Herodias, on returning home, found herself vaguely comparing Herod with her own spouse Philip. She reached the conclusion that the odds were all against Philip. She made up her mind that Herod was going to be her man.

She judged, and correctly, that he would be easy prey. Just the same she laid her plans carefully, played every card at the right moment and won every trick. Came the day when Herod opened wide his great hall door to admit Herodias and her child. He closed the door behind them. This time they had come to stay.

Most people in the company were too prudent and far too polite to pretend they had noticed anything, still less to breathe a syllable of censure when either of the guilty couple might be within earshot. This sort of thing was not done — in good society. Besides, they depended on the prince's favor after all for the pleasant living they enjoyed under Herod's hospitable roof. So why bother? It was none of their business.

Plain Talk

After that things began to settle down quite nicely. The situation had come to be taken for granted. But now at this point we have to introduce a meddlesome intruder, one of these "do-gooders" who can be such an insufferable nuisance. He breaks in here on the story, uncouth, ill-mannered, unconventional, upsetting the harmony, destroying all the fun. John was his name; he was commonly known as the Baptizer. He appeared like an apparition from another world, suddenly let down into the midst of the splendor and luxury and all the vice that lay heavy on the atmosphere in this place.

The black hair on his head was long and dishevelled. His thick growth of beard hid most of his face but threw into more glaring relief his eyes, which flashed fire. He was clothed in camel's hair and wore a girdle around his waist. He arrived, unexpected, unannounced, uninvited, and certainly unwelcome, direct from Jordan, on a self-imposed mission. From what he had been telling the audiences who gathered to listen to him at the riverbank, it was clear that this John was a fearless man and transparently sincere. His message was concise, down-to-earth, with no trimmings to make it more palatable, couched in words that nobody could fail to understand. "Do penance," he cried. "Brood of vipers, who warned you to flee from the retribution that is coming? . . . I baptize you with water. The one who comes after me will baptize you with the Holy Spirit and with fire. The wheat he will gather into his barn; the chaff he will burn in unquenchable fire."

So today in this stuffy, evil-smelling banquet hall, this man of God, ignoring all introductions and explanations, singles out the one person to whom his message is most pertinent. He walks the full length of the room, stands right in front of the king, who by this time is sodden and stupified from having drunk too much. John makes no bow or salutation. He is far too honest a man to feign a respect he does not feel. As at the Jordan, so here too, he goes straight to the point. Indicating Herod unmistakably with the accusing index finger of his right hand, he speaks one single, brief sentence. "It is not lawful for you," he tells Herod, "to have your brother's wife."

These few words seem to rock the entire palace. The air becomes electrified. The audience is first speechless with astonishment, then furious and indignant that they should witness such an outrage. Who is this creature, so wanting in tact, so grossly discourteous, as to address ugly expressions like these to anyone at any time, but more especially to such a person, in his own house and in such company?

Meantime John has not moved an inch. He still continues

to look steadily into the shifting eyes of Herod, oblivious of the comments buzzing around his ears. He has said all he wants to say. To add emphasis to his statement and to remove all possible doubt as to whom he had spoken, he stretches out his right hand full in the direction of the miserable man he has censured, as though to say, "It's *you!*"

Reactions

What a bear the fellow is! By now the horrified guests are all chattering together. The air vibrates with protests, with expressions of sympathy, with demands that this ignorant lout be made, there and then, to pay for his insolence to his betters. And as for poor distressed Herodias, this reflection on herself and the man she loves is the unkindest cut of all. Her lady friends, deeply concerned, flock around her and do what they can to comfort her. She turns to Herod with streaming eyes. She looks pleadingly at him and suggests that this fanatic who has come between them is a menace to society. Better lock him up. Ostensibly it was a request, but Herod knew in his heart that it was an order he must not dare disobey. So he sent John to prison. He had long since become her lackey. Such a judge!

John remained under arrest, locked up in his cell, for nearly four months. Herod often came to speak to him. In his heart he had respect for this man who did not hesitate to tell him the truth. It was quite a novelty for the king to get the truth, accustomed as he was to listening to lies and sham, which, in his rare lucid moments, left him feeling rather sick. But John was every inch a man, afraid of no one — except God for whom fear was an expression of love. Herod confessed interiorly to having a feeling of envy for this intrepid apostle and his courage, especially when he viewed this against the background of his own superficial existence.

He used to feel better for these talks with John, for he saw that he was a truly good and holy man. When he heard him speak he was greatly perplexed, for the attitude of the Baptist to life was beyond his powers of comprehension, and yet we are told "he liked to listen to him." But he was the plaything of his emotions, this man Herod, and we learn that at other times he felt inclined to kill John. He did not dare do so, "because he was afraid of the people who regarded him as a prophet."

Meantime Herodias, "like a tigress, would watch for her opportunity, and, when the occasion came, like a tigress she would spring." She found it on the king's birthday. Another party, of course, and Salome, her daughter, danced before Herod and his assembled visitors. They were spellbound. When finally she came to a halt and bowed herself out, Antipas lifted his right hand and swore an oath. "Marvelous! Ask whatever you want and it is yours, even half my kingdom." Coached in advance by her unscrupulous mother, the girl replied at once: "What I would like is the head of John the Baptist on a dish." The king was struck dumb. In his drunken stupor he had never foreseen such a possible request. He would like to turn it down, but then there was his solemn oath. And if he went back on what he had promised, what would his grand guests think and say? He must be a man of his word!

Salome got what she asked for, the head of the Baptist in a dish, dripping blood. She gave it to her mother. The tigress drew a long breath, her thirst sated at last.

Such a Prisoner!

But the degradation deepens. It would be humiliating enough for any common criminal to be tried by a judge with Herod's record for vice. But when that "criminal" is Jesus Christ we can find no words forceful enough, comprehensive enough, graphic enough, to express the reality. Such a judge and such a prisoner!

Early on that Good Friday morning a messenger knocked on the door of the palace of Herod, stating that he had an important document from Pontius Pilate. He was admitted at once. He has been instructed to say that his master would have King Herod know that a slighty demented Galilean was at large and causing a lot of trouble. He comes from Nazareth. Jesus is his name. He is charged on some points of Jewish law, and Pilate realized that Herod would have a competence to deal with these that Pilate himself did not possess. Would he be willing to handle the case and decide what should be done?

The tetrarch was highly gratified. Never before had the Roman condescended to him like this. Ordinarily, he practically ignored his existence. The two had had a falling-out — no one could be long in contact with the governor and manage to maintain friendly relations with him. This request about Jesus should help to bridge the chasm. Worldliness and wickedness usually travel amicably enough along the same road. "And though Herod and Pilate had been enemies before, they were reconciled that same day" (Luke 23:12). But Herod was even more thrilled at the prospect of meeting Jesus. For over a year he had been listening to amazing stories about him. There was compelling evidence, he was assured, that Jesus had cleansed lepers, changed water into wine, restored sight to the blind and hearing to the deaf, had summoned a man out of his grave who had been four days dead. At first these reports struck terror into the heart of the king. This must be the Baptist, he reflected, the man I beheaded, now returned to this world to be avenged on me. He was haunted by the thought. He grew morose and silent. But as the months passed on and nothing untoward happened, the fear wore off and he began to breathe again. He was now, rather, consumed with curiosity to see this magician, watch him performing some of his tricks, perhaps learn from him how to do them himself.

At the very least, he could look forward to a pleasant interview. Jesus is here now, on the doorstep. The word spread around, and the whole household came together to see the fun. They stood or sat or squatted, wherever they could find room. Herod was seated in his own special armchair. Jesus was shown in and stood before him. The king was in a state of glee, which he could not suppress. So this was, really and truly, the far-famed Jesus of Nazareth. Herod had heard so much about the wisdom of the words he spoke and the secret knowledge he seemed to possess. Would he not share some of these good things with them here this morning? suggested Herod. Then there were some interesting problems which had been agitating his mind for quite a while. Herod would like to propose them and hear what Jesus thought about them. Most of all there was his skill as a magician, which they all were hoping he would display.

Let Jesus show Himself cooperative and Herod would reward Him, might even regain His freedom for Him. It was now His turn to speak and act. Dead silence followed. The prisoner stood there before His judge, stood in His strong manly way, looking into those cowering eyes without fear, without respect. "That fox," He had called him one day. Jesus had spoken to Caiaphas and Pilate and Annas, for in these, despite their wickedness, there was still left some remnant of humanity. But there was no better self in Herod. He was a monster of iniquity, and he was quite complacent about it. The maddening silence continued. The stillness was becoming unendurable.

As on another occasion, "Jesus held his peace." He seems unconscious of even the presents of the mob surrounding him. They are ignored. They seem almost not to exist. The prisoner is showing contempt of court, a slur, a totally unexpected anticlimax.

Such a Sentence!

Such a judge and such a prisoner; what a glaring contrast! Christ, who had said: "Which of you will convict me of sin?" And no one dared accept the challenge. And Herod, creature of the gutter, authorized to pronounce sentence upon him! Herod is taken aback. He never expected contempt like this from the countryman from Nazareth. He is painfully aware that he is being made to look rather like a fool, and in the presence of all these people too. His pride is hurt. What can he do to save face? Yes. he has an idea. Christ has made him look like a fool. Now he would be hoist with his own petard.

Herod beckons to a slave, who advances and kneels for instructions. He rises, bows, retires and presently returns, carrying a tray on which a white garment lies folded. The king stands up, waits till he is sure of the attention of them all, smiles and lifts the cloak off the tray. Put this poor harmless imbecile to death? Ah, no! Herod had some humanity left in him still. He takes the white garment, holds it daintily between thumb and forefinger of each hand, sidles over to Christ and bows in mock reverence, then moves behind and throws it across his shoulders.

Brilliant! An instantaneous transformation in the atmosphere! Herod's act was a masterstroke. The white cloak indicated that Christ was a fool. They knew it, and they were quick to take the cue. The tactful thing now was to play up to the mood of their master and restore him to good humor. They roared with laughter. They gave him a standing ovation. The applause was deafening, but "Jesus held his peace."

Herod sent Christ back to Pilate, to walk through the public streets, a curious and interesting exhibit for the people to laugh at.

Herod now returned to his reveling, his wine and women and dancing and feasting and song. The jarring note was soon forgotten. The unpleasant incident rubbed off and was never mentioned again, at least if the monarch was near. With Jesus Herod had felt very much as when he was confronted with the Baptizer. On both occasions conscience spoke, if only in a faint whisper. On the whole he felt rather depressed by this latest experience. Christ's grace appeals and warns but never forces. Herod tried to forget. He succeeded. It is dreadfully possible for all of us to do the same.

Pope Paul VI

Herod made fun of the purity of Christ. Men in the Seventies ridicule Pope Paul because he warns us about the widespread prevalence of "aberrant sex." He stresses the purpose of sex — a power given by God to man and woman whereby to people this world for a time and heaven for all eternity. This power may be used only for the purpose intended by God and only by persons joined together in lawful wedlock. The Church feels acutely for persons for whom the observance of God's law in this matter presents a special difficulty. She teaches that He will certainly offer grace sufficient to cope with this situation if those concerned take the means to obtain it. If she is mocked at for her doctrine she remembers the jeers of Herod and the silence of Christ.

THE DRAMA

THE DRAMA

HE WALKED THIS WAY

So far we have sketched the character and background of the different actors. We shall now watch them as they move in and out, each one to fulfill his role in the different episodes of the great story.

Like them, we too have an active part to play, as one scene after another unfolds itself before us, all of them combining to lead us up to the climax on Calvary. There is a long-standing tradition in the Church, which we have no difficulty in accepting. It is assumed that, many times after the Resurrection, Our Lady and the apostles and the holy women used to walk in the footsteps of Christ along the route from Pilate's house to the place where Jesus had been crucified. Anything to the contrary would have been incredible. They would have made the journey slowly and prayerfully, delaying at those places where some outstanding incident had happened — where His Mother had met Him, where He had fallen, where Simon had come to His assistance, where He consoled the group of women who wept in sympathy. Most of all would they have lingered at the spot where He was crucified, seeing again the nails and the blood and the spittle and the agonizing look, and listening once more to the words He had spoken.

They would have gone down to the place where He had been buried, just as we visit the graves of those we love. They did not pray for Him as we pray; they prayed *to* Him. Nor did they find His body there, as we find what we call so aptly "the remains" of our friends and relatives. An angel had asked on Easter morning: "Why do you seek for the living among the dead? He is not here. He is risen."

Way of the Cross

From this tradition has developed the practice of making the Stations, or of following the Way of the Cross. The first beginnings of the devotion are obscure. In the fifth century the bishop of Bologna set up a group of chapels in the monastery of St. Stephen, each containing a shrine depicting one of the principal events of the Passion. There are records, too, written by several pilgrims, who visited the holy places during the early centuries. They describe a fixed route which had come to be regarded as the road actually traveled by Our Lord. The word "stations" is first applied to the different halting places by William Wey, an Englishman who went to Palestine in 1458.

Round about this same period many sets of stations were erected in different places throughout Europe. Blessed Father Alvarez, a Dominican, on returning from Jerusalem, built a series of little shrines in his friary at Cordoba, in each of which were painted scenes showing the principal events of the Passion. A Poor Clare nun did the same soon after in her convent at Messina. A famous Way of the Cross was built at Fribourg in 1507, and another at Varallo by the Franciscans, whose guardian, Blessed Bernardino Caini, had been custodian of the holy places. In many of these early works an attempt was made not only to reproduce the scenes as accurately as possible, but to space them from each other the exact same distance as was shown in the original. It was considered that the fervor of those people who made the stations would be helped if they realized they were covering the same amount of ground as had been traversed by Christ.

Since that distant period the custom of erecting the stations has become so widespread that there is scarcely a church that does not possess them. The devotion has been lavishly enriched with indulgences by the Church, the same indulgences which could formerly be gained only by going in person to the holy places.

This is clear evidence of the high esteem in which the Church holds the stations and her deep concern that the practice of "making" them should flourish among Catholics everywhere. There is no more effective way of obeying Christ's command to take up our cross and follow Him. There is no religious exercise calculated to impress on us more deeply the tremendous truths to be drawn from the Passion and inflame our hearts with a personal love for Jesus crucified. It has a vital part to play in our apostolate to bring Christ back.

Ourselves

We write this the more earnestly because we know that a modern shibboleth would persuade us that this devotion is dated and belongs to a generation that is dead or dying. If this were true it would account in large measure for the mediocrity and apostasy we see around us. It would help to explain the sickening of a virile, living faith that has pervaded the Church. If we are to bring Christ back, this is where we begin. If this book would contribute even a little to fan the flame of love of the Passion, in the hearts of those who read it, the author would bless God in time and in eternity.

Listen to St. Paul's words, throbbing with anxiety and affection for his converts in Philippi: "If our life in Christ means anything to you; if love can persuade at all, or the Spirit that we have in common, or any tenderness or sympathy, then be united in your convictions, be united in your love" (Philippians 2:1). This means to say he is longing and praying for the day when he will see their minds undergoing a profound change. To win control of the mind is the sure way to bend another to one's will, for good or for evil. What will transform us into men and women of God is not merely an abundance of theories and principles, however sound in themselves, but to feel, to experience, to come to grips with living truth, to taste it and relish it in mind and heart.

"Let this mind be in you which was also in Christ Jesus."
How is this to be done? Unquestionably by walking frequently
and prayerfully with Jesus and Mary to Calvary. One would like
to suggest, for a start, "a station a day." Give five or six minutes
to that one station alone and pass by the rest. This should prove
immensely more helpful to one's spiritual life than to hurry
around from one station to another with the idea of getting
through. In what follows we have drawn up, tentatively and as a
suggestion, a program that may help us. The material provided
for our prayerful meditation at each station is divided up into
sections. Each section contains one idea drawn from the particular scene we are witnessing. At the end of each station there is
printed a "keyword," a summary of what has gone before. One
word, into which is compressed one thought; thought and word
both evolved from one station at a time. This may lead us to talk
very simply with Jesus and Mary. Or we may just want to stand
or kneel or sit and look at the scene before us. A station a day if
you wish, but really "make" it. Try this for once a week by way
of start. By degrees you may get around to doing it every day.
Fidelity to this simple program is bound to help us develop the
mind of Christ in us.

There are some powerfully moving events in the Passion
which are not included in the stations. These we propose to contemplate together before beginning the journey to Calvary. Also,
we are going to add on a fifteenth station on the Resurrection, as
we gratefully acknowledge we are now permitted to do. There is
a "setting" at the beginning of each scene, which is intended to
help us steady our imagination.

THE AGONY IN THE GARDEN

Setting: About eleven o'clock at night in the garden of olives. The moon is shining through the branches of the trees, and in the broken light I discern the figure of Jesus in prayer. When first I catch sight of Him He is kneeling upright with hands joined, but as I continue to watch He falls flat on His face, extends both arms full on the ground, and His whole body begins to writhe in anguish. Again He lifts Himself to a kneeling posture. This time the moon's rays fall across His face, and I see that His eyes are stark with terror. He stretches out His hands, and the tense silence is broken with His cry of agony. Here I kneel in spirit, alone with Him, close to Him, for there is material here for many an hour of prayerful meditation.

First Section

What first impresses me is the aloneness of Christ. He has left His three friends a little distance away and has plunged into the darkness and solitude to give Himself to prayer. This hour He had foreseen and had looked forward to it with dread. "Listen," He had told them. "The time will come — in fact it is here already — when you will be scattered, each going his own way and leaving me alone." Here in Gethsemani He is embarking on a hand-to-hand struggle with Satan. There is stillness. There is an atmosphere of expectancy. One senses that something ominous is afoot and Christ must grapple with it, with no human support to sustain Him, with no friend to speak a word of encouragement. "I have trodden the winepress alone. . . . I sought for one that would grieve together with me and there was none. . . .".

There are many who have had and are having this same experience. Climb up the rickety stairs. Open the door on the landing. Enter and find yourself in a dark dingy little room. Lying in bed is a poor old woman, blind and in her eighties. Who cares? You are the first visitor she has had for two days. She understands the loneliness of Christ.

How many are alone because someone they loved has been done to death by violence? How many will tell you they have no friends? Said one of them in my hearing: "Live as long as you can, and when you cannot live just drop down and die, and nobody cares!"

And yet loneliness can be a blessing. It can transport the soul into a new world and make it largely independent of this one. There are men serving a twenty-year sentence, perhaps a life sentence, in prison, and the aloneness, when once they learned how to accept it, transformed them into saints.

Keyword: ALONENESS

Second Section

There is much to comfort us in the thought that Christ, in the hour of His aloneness, was human enough to seek human sympathy. Three of His chosen friends were not far away, so He got up off His knees, walked out from under the trees and came to them in His distress. But they proved to be broken reeds. Their eyes were heavy with sleep, and we have it from the gospel account itself that they did not have a word to say to Him. He went back to His prayer. He returned to them a second and a third time, disappointed each time, and each time left alone in His aloneness.

He continued to pray. "And being in an agony, he prayed the longer." And now strength and consolation came from another source, and this new presence banished, or at least mitigated, the feeling of aloneness that had oppressed Him. One finds it extraordinarily moving to see God begging sympathy from His creatures and accepting it gratefully.

So we are by no means forbidden to turn to our human friends for consolation when we find ourselves sharing in the aloneness of Christ. We are fortunate indeed if we have a friend who, we know, is genuinely interested, who will take time to listen to us, to advise and help us to a solution. But most people cannot be bothered. They have their own worries. They have other friends more interesting and entertaining than we can hope to be. So we are gracefully bowed out, and the insinuation that we are not expected back is unmistakably conveyed.

Is this not just what happened to Christ in the hour of His aloneness? "Their eyes were heavy, and they did not know what to say to him." This thought, if we can keep it in mind, will at once stifle all feelings of resentment, of wounded pride, of bitterness, when we are let down by our human friend in our hour of need.

What should our reactions be is clear from His example. He left them, went back to His solitude and aloneness, "and prayed the longer, saying the selfsame words." A priest visited a poor woman who was suffering from two cancers, one on each breast. She told him she was the happiest woman in the parish!

Keyword: CONSOLATION

Third Section

Jesus spoke, figuratively, of His "chalice." As I kneel beside Him let me take it into my hands. On looking into it I find it has three bitter ingredients. The first is fear. "He began to be afraid." No wonder, since, as St. John tells us, He knew everything that was going to happen to Him. With strained eyes He peers into the darkness and sees the procession of horrors awaiting Him in the immediate future. He shrinks back in terror from the vision of the scourging, the crowning with thorns, the journey made to the place of crucifixion, the weight of the cross, the cries of derision, the nails, the three hours.

"He began to be afraid." If we know the anticipation of a major critical operation we shall have a faint idea of the fear of Christ. Christ prayed that the chalice might pass from Him, but His prayer was not answered. This is good to remember when we beg to be spared an ordeal and again, apparently, we pray in vain.

The second ingredient in this chalice I am holding is disgust. A specter emerges from the shadows, the name of which is sin, and His immaculate being experiences an overpowering feeling of loathing. Who can understand sin? Certainly not sinful men, for passion blinds us to its malice. "Man, when he was in honor, did not understand; he compared himself to the brute beasts and became as one of them." But Christ understands sin, and the sight of its heinousness forces the blood out through the pores of His body. There is a third ingredient — sadness. "My soul," He confesses, "is sorrowful even to death." Despite all He is going to suffer, souls will remain obdurate in sin. All through this book we keep coming back to the fact of His personal love for each one of us. That is why even one mortal sin pierces His heart with sorrow. What, then, if there was a sea of such sins?

Keyword: INGREDIENTS

Fourth Section

His friends failed Him that night. And His enemies? Their camp on that same night was a hive of energy. Judas is alert to seize on this opportunity to collect his blood money. Annas, an old man, forgets his need of sleep. Caiaphas, the high priest, wants no rest. While Christ's enemies are busy and vigilant His friends are asleep. Has history repeated itself in the Seventies?

Keyword: ASLEEP?

THE SCOURGING AT THE PILLAR

Setting: In the barrackyard at the back of Pilate's house. The hands of Christ are tied together with a piece of rope, which runs through an iron ring at the top of the pillar. The pillar is a high one, a foot or two higher than Christ Himself. So they have to raise His arms above His head and regulate the length of the rope in such a way that only the tips of His toes touch the ground. Being thus deprived of His feet, He suffers more. They beat Him mercilessly, on whatever part of His body the lash chances to fall. Did He allow even a groan to escape Him? The prophet has written that He did not open His mouth. They cut the ropes at last, and Jesus collapses at the foot of the pillar. I am on my knees, of course, for this is holy ground. Lying over there in His own blood, He forces His eyes open to look across at me. Prayer in such circumstances should not be difficult.

First Section

There is, first of all, the *cruelty* of the scourging. There are weighty reasons for supposing that it was, in fact, inhumanly cruel. First of all the prophecy had to be fulfilled that "from the sole of the foot to the top of the head" there would be "no soundness therein." Nowhere else in the Passion does this seem to be fulfilled except in this scourging.

There is also the fact of Pilate's motive in ordering this scourging. He was at his wits' end, and to save this innocent man he wanted Him to be reduced to such a pitiable state that the sight of Him would certainly soften the bronze hearts of those who are demanding His death — and by crucifixion. So he would have warned the soldiers not to let Him off lightly. In point of fact they scarcely needed the warning. Jewish law had laid down regulations to control the punishment of criminals condemned to be scourged. The number of strokes was limited; a judge had always to preside, and those who inflicted the scourging were reminded that even a criminal was a human being. No matter how black his crime, he still deserved some measure of respect. But there was nothing like this written into Roman law, and anyhow Jesus was only a Jew from despised Nazareth. No one was going to bother what they did with Him, so they might with impunity vent their cruelty and hatred just as much as they liked.

It is significant, too, that the evangelists refrain from any detailed description of the scourging. All they say is: "Then Pilate took Jesus and scourged him." If Christ suffered like this for my sins is it much that I, like Him, accept the hard things of life in a spirit of expiation?

Keyword: CRUELTY

Second Section

The scourging was also appallingly *unjust*. Twice over the governor had publicly stated that the prisoner was an innocent man. "I find no cause in him; no, nor Herod either. I will chastise him, *therefore*, and let him go." Was there ever a more illogical "therefore" uttered? Shift the scene for a moment to a modern courthouse. The prisoner is in the dock. All the evidence has been produced. The jury retires and returns in due course with a verdict, "not guilty." The prisoner smiles and sighs with relief and looks down to his delighted wife and children and sees them waving congratulations. The judge rises and tells the court: "This man has been examined and tried, and the jury declares that he is innocent. I have decided, therefore, to sentence him to two years' imprisonment!"

Fantastic? Well, consider. Jesus had healed the sick, had consoled the lonely and the depressed. "I will chastise Him, therefore..." No charge has been proved against Him; He has done all things well. He challenged His enemies to point to a single sin in His whole life; they could not do it. "Therefore, let Him be scourged!"

With that "therefore" ringing in our ears and written in our hearts we may well decide that it is better to forgive than to vindicate, better to be silent about the wrongs received than break out into complaints, better to remain under a cloud of misunderstanding and wait for God to dispel the mist when and as He sees fit.

Keyword: THEREFORE

Third Section

Christ is still lying over there in a pool of blood, more dead than alive, at the base of the pillar. His mouth is wide open; this makes His breathing a little less difficult. Each breath is audible; any one breath might prove to be His last. His two rows of white teeth show against His black beard. His long hair, clotted with blood, hangs disheveled over His shoulders. His persecutors regard the spectacle with some concern, not any remote feeling of sympathy or compassion, but alarm lest the prisoner should die. They had been given strict orders not to kill Him. It would be bad news for them if it was found that they had exceeded their table of reference.

The Passion of Christ was a great exorcism. Satan had taken possession of the human race. By succeeding in making us sin he had darkened our minds and corrupted our hearts and weakened our wills in their determination to do good. If the world is to be exorcised the exorcism can be performed only by a person whose soul has never been touched by the least stain of sin. Here at the pillar we see Jesus performing this exorcism and the price it is costing Him. When two friends have a difference of opinion, which culminates, let us suppose, in a bitter quarrel, reconciliation will be difficult, perhaps impossible, to bring about.

This does not happen in the work of the divine Exorcist. God forgives and forgets absolutely and forever. He assures us Himself that He will "no more remember" our sins. He has put them all behind His back; He has cast them into the depths of the sea.

Keyword: EXORCISM

THE CORONATION

Setting: Still in the barrackyard of Pilate's palace. The soldiers now drag Jesus from the place He has been lying since the scourging had ended. At this stage He is already a dying, tottering man, even though what has transpired so far is only chapter one in the volume containing the entire story of His sufferings. He can scarcely stand. Reluctantly they take hold of His arms, one on the right and one on the left and between them they bundle Him along to the throne prepared for Him. It is a low stool. He stumbles over it because the blood and tears have blinded His eyes. This is our great high priest, waiting for His attendants to robe Him and vest Him and accompany Him in solemn procession to the altar for Mass. I can see and hear everything from the corner of the room where I am kneeling. The spectacle is heartrending, but mighty in its potential to win me to the love of Christ.

First Section

They bring the celebrant His vestment, His chasuble. The color is scarlet. They place it over His head and let it slip down over His shoulders and body. In a very few minutes it is sodden in blood. His clothes were saturated like this three times in the course of His Passion — in the garden where they were the expression of His *obedience*; here at the pillar where they are a reminder of *chastity*; and on Calvary where, deprived even of them, He preaches and practices complete *poverty*.

Keyword: VESTMENTS

Second Section

The high priest must have His miter. "Hath He diadem as
monarch that His brow adorns? Yes, a crown in very surety, but
of thorns." They do not merely lay it on His head; to make certain it will stay in position they beat the thorns into place. It was
probably shaped like a cap, covering the entire surface of the
head of Christ. This crown is of no commercial value. When finally He lays it down it will be dumped on the garbage heap, a
symbol of the contempt in which He holds all earthly crowns.

He has His vestments and His miter. All He needs now is
His crozier and the procession will be able to move off toward
the altar. For crozier they put a reed in His hand — another
cheap jibe to mock His pretensions. The Pontiff on His throne,
complete with vestments, miter and crozier. Can I catch the echo
of what He said on another occasion? "Wonder not if the world
hates you. If you had been of the world the world would love its
own. But because you are not of the world, but I have chosen
you out of the world, therefore the world hates you."

Keyword: HIGH PRIEST

Third Section

A solemn ritual has now to be performed before priest and minis-
ters proceed to the altar. They stand before Him and bow head
and shoulders in homage. They bend the right knee till it touches
the ground. This Satan-inspired liturgy is drawn up with one object in view — to heap on Christ every insult that can be devised.
They come close to Him and look leeringly into His face. He
can feel their foul breath upon Him. They struck His face; they
spat upon it; they blindfolded Him. I suppose there is no gesture
so expressive of contempt as to spit deliberately into a person's
face. And did they blindfold Him because they could not endure
the contrast between the limpid purity shining in those eyes and

their own depravity? By now His chasuble is dripping blood, so they decide to take it off and give it back to its owner. To Christ they restore the garment "seamless, woven in one piece, from neck to hem." Likely it was made for Him by Mary, His Mother, as many a mother since has made a set of vestments for the first Mass of her priest-son.

Keyword: RITUAL

Fourth Section

The parody we have been witnessing is with us today. It is known as the Black Mass. It is inspired by a satanic hatred of Christ. It is celebrated by persons who believe in the Real Presence. Its debauchery rivals the insults and blasphemies of Pilate's barrackyard.

Why introduce it here? Because we Catholics have inherited what Newman calls "the garment of affliction." When the prophet Elijah was about to leave this world "a chariot of fire appeared ... and took him to heaven." His cloak fell on the shoulders of his disciple Elisha, who inherited with it the "double spirit" of his master.

When Christ went up to heaven His garment fell on the members of His Church, and every true follower of His must wear it. It means that when we are "afflicted" with orgies like the Black Mass, we respond to the challenge by prayer and penance and apostolic zeal.

Keyword: BLACK MASS

FIRST STATION:
JESUS CONDEMNED

Setting: Hoffman has given us a picture of Christ before Pilate. He is still "fairest among the sons of men." The beauty of His face has not yet been marred with blood and spittle. His eyes look piercingly into the eyes of His judge. He is fearless but not defiant; majestic but not proud; respectful of Pilate's authority but not cringing; wanting no favors; asking only for a fair trial, an impartial judge, a just jury, a sentence based on truth. He stands there erect, holding His head high, fearing no man. It is difficult to recognize Him for the same man after the scourging. Sin has made the difference.

First Section

His mental sufferings as He stands there probably cause Him more anguish than the physical pains in His body. There is, first, His sense of the galling *injustice* done to Him. "What evil has he done?" Pilate had asked the mob in the courtyard below. They trumped up one charge after another, each of which, on being investigated, was proved to be false. Christ was an innocent man; therefore let Him be crucified. He has done no evil; therefore let Him be scourged. He has done all things well; therefore let us spit in His face.

The terrific strength of Christ? How a single gesture of impatience would mar the beauty of this scene? There are many in our day, in concentration camps, on beds of sickness, existing in squalor and inhuman conditions, and they have learned from Christ the lesson of silent endurance. Theirs is "the folly of the cross," which seals their lips. They are heartened as often as they remember that in this first station "Jesus held His peace."

Keyword: INJUSTICE

Second Section

Jesus turns His eyes away from Pilate and looks down at the seething mass of humanity in the street below. A few days ago some of these were probably in the procession into Jerusalem when they made the streets echo with their cries of Hosanna. What a glaring contrast today! He wept even on Palm Sunday because He clearly saw they had missed the whole purpose of His coming. Now, from His place beside Pilate, He sees how insane hatred has taken over and nothing will satisfy it except His death. Down there stands Mary His Mother, and John and Magdalene. Nothing could ever separate them from Him or Him from them. The minds of all the others have been poisoned against Him.

"Those friends thou hast and their adoption tried, grapple them to thy soul with hoops of steel." But in this station we see that to depend too much on human friendship is to build one's house on sand. There is a false friendship, which easily degenerates into mere expediency.

Keyword: INGRATITUDE

Third Section

At any moment Christ could have torn the mask of hypocrisy from the faces of His enemies. He could have frozen their hearts with terror by shedding His crown of thorns, instantly closing His wounds, casting off the tawdry purple and showing Himself as He did in the glory of His Transfiguration. In our impetuous zeal we almost wish He had done something like this.

What is the secret of this perfect serenity, this amazing self-mastery? All through His Passion He is looking uninterruptedly into the beauty of the face of His Father. This more than compensates for His sufferings. We, too, see our God now by faith, and soon "as He is in Himself." That assurance brings us a peace which the world does not know.

Keyword: SERENITY

SECOND STATION:
CARRYING THE CROSS

Setting: The procession now moves away from Pilate's house, through the streets of the city, to the altar to be set up on Calvary for the high priest's Mass. I see the executioners, ignorant of who Christ was, who were there just on a routine job. There are the Jews who hated Him; people who were led by mere curiosity to see what was going to happen; there were His faithful friends, Mary, Magdalene, John, and probably a few others. To which group do *I* belong? A vitally important question, which I must answer before I set out. If I have sinned and repented there is Magdalene to encourage me. If, through God's grace I have preserved my baptismal innocence, my place is with John, "the disciple whom Jesus loved." In either case I can feel at home with Mary. If she is queen of saints, she is also refuge of sinners.

First Section

Sometimes a cross was set up permanently in the ground at the place of crucifixion, and the condemned man did not have to carry it. This did not happen in the case of Christ. "Bearing his own cross," writes St. John, who was there, "he went forth." The transverse beam measured about six feet across; the longer beam was twice that length. Christ must have quailed at the prospect of carrying such a weight, especially in His exhausted state. It would have presented grave difficulties for even a man in his prime, for the cross was unwieldy, the streets were narrow, and making progress was particularly difficult at this precise season when thousands of visitors had poured into the city and continually jammed the procession. Ordinarily the journey could be made in a quarter of an hour. In Our Lord's case it must have taken at least a full hour.

Note, too, that the immense concourse of strangers added much to His humiliation. "He humbled himself, even to the death of the cross." It was "His own" cross. Every detail has been prearranged; He reaches out both hands and accepts it. "His own" cross. If only I had any other cross than the one *I* have to bear . . .!

Keyword: His OWN Cross

Second Section

The first reaction to the cross is undisguised rejection. Those who adopt it are out for money and a good time. When, to these, a thorn-crowned, bleeding Christ presents Himself and invites them to share His cross, they stare at Him in blank amazement, perhaps even with contempt. For these, suffering in any form is an unmitigated misfortune, a most unwelcome visitor if it lands on their doorstep, to be dismissed at once without ceremony or apology.

The second class are resigned to the cross. They will put up with it because it cannot be avoided. This is much, but do the saints stop short at mere resignation? Does Christ in this station? *Acceptance* is the acid test.

Keyword: ATTITUDES

Third Section

A blind man cannot watch TV. A man who is stone deaf cannot enjoy the symphony concert. They both lack receptivity. Selfishness, in its myriad forms, dims our vision of the beauty and worth of sanctity. It lessens our capacity to receive the gifts God wants to give us. Selfishness makes us unresponsive when God speaks in our heart about the needs of the apostolate. Christ is the divine physician, and He comes with the remedy in His hands to put right this deplorable situation. It is "the cross of Our Lord Jesus Christ, in whom is salvation, life, and resurrection, through whom we are saved and set at liberty." "By means of sufferings the soul arrives at great holiness and a close imitation of the Son of God. . . . Thence arise favors and heavenly secrets, known only to Him and the soul which receives them. . . ." This language of the saints gives us insight into the significance of this second station.

Keyword: RECEPTIVITY

THIRD STATION:
THE FIRST FALL

Setting: It is safe to conclude that Our Lord fell, and oftener than three times. There is a tradition that the soldiers tied His arms to the transverse beam to make sure the cross would not slip. If this was so He did not have His hands to help Him break the fall. His face struck the hard pavement. Blood spurted out from His open mouth and nostrils. His teeth were loosened, some of them probably broken. At one point along the route there is an incline, reaching down rather steeply into a ravine. This is considered to be the spot where He fell for the first time. Let me close over this book for a little while and take time to look and try to realize. That man, lying there flat on His face, with the cross on His shoulders pressing Him into the ground — who is He and why is He there?

First Section

Very commonly when we fall on our knees or prostrate ourselves on the ground, we do it in order to pray. The magi at Bethlehem, "falling on their knees, did him homage." A leper met Christ one day, "and seeing Jesus, fell on his face and implored him. . . ." We can safely assume that Our Lord is offering this first fall as a prayer to His Father. It is a prayer of *adoration*, united with these blessed spirits who "prostrate themselves before God's throne and sing a new hymn of praise." Christ's prayer as He lies there is, secondly, the expression of a *desire* that the whole world would understand His Passion and come to the knowledge of the truth. It is an *offering* of all His sufferings in atonement to the outraged majesty of His heavenly Father. Finally it is a *plea* that His offering might be accepted.

Is it difficult to kneel in spirit beside Him and repeat, over and over again, the acts that constitute His prayer in this first fall?

Keyword: The PRAYER of Christ

Second Section

Can I recall my own first fall, the time and circumstances under which I committed my first mortal sin? I was young, old, or middle-aged. I was alone or with a companion, married or single, at home or abroad. Anyhow it was my first grievous sin, and the fact that I had done it shocked me to the depths of my soul. Even now it has the appearance of a hideous specter issuing from the shadows of the past.

Father Claude Liseur, Jesuit missionary, said on his deathbed: "I'm eighty-two, and, thanks to God's infinite mercy and the help of Our Lady, I can truthfully say that never, in eighty-two years, did I offend my God by a mortal sin." Claude Liseur had no "first fall." "Blessed are the clear of heart for they shall see God." All this supplies material for conversation with Christ, according as the Holy Spirit will give me to speak.

Keyword: LISEUR

Third Section

All sin is a falling down in worship before an idol. In the case of the pharisees the idol was hardness of heart and *self-righteousness*. This is illustrated by the utter callousness with which they dragged before Christ the poor woman whom they "caught" in the very act of committing adultery. This is the besetting sin of religious people. Surely Christ prayed for them during His first fall. *Money*, another idol, changed Judas from a disciple into a traitor. Pilate was a slave to *worldliness* and Herod to *sensuality*.

"I am the Lord, your God; you shall not have strange gods before Me." Are there any such strange gods in my life?

Did Christ wish, humanly speaking, to stay down? Let them allow Him to remain here and die in peace. He would have cast away the idea and by doing so turned apparent failure into victory.

Keyword: IDOLS

FOURTH STATION: MOTHER AND SON

Setting: It would be unthinkable that this meeting should not have taken place. Mary had probably spent the night in the home of Martha and Mary Magdalene in Bethania. She would surely have heard, in the early morning, that Jesus had been seized and imprisoned. Peter and John would have arrived in the small hours and broken the news to her. She thanked them and, one would surmise, then retired into her room and prayed to her Father in secret. Later in the day John called for her, accompanied her to a spot where the procession would pass, and they waited for Him there.

First Section

There is, first of all, the *courage* of Mary. It is foreshadowed in the story of the mother of the Maccabees, which you should certainly read in the seventh chapter of the second book bearing that title. Her seven sons were put to death with savage cruelty while she encouraged them to constancy, and last of all she died herself for the law of God.

We do not have to decide which of these two mothers had the greater courage. Today, Good Friday, the courage of Our Lady will be put to its most demanding test, and she will not falter. "God spared not his only Son," and that Son did not spare His own loved Mother.

Keyword: COURAGE

Second Section

"Jesus," writes St. Ignatius, "spent the whole of that night in bonds." There was no admission. One guard had to remain on duty while his companions shuffled off to bed. So there was no admission to the prisoner's cell. But there was a window outside, through which the moonlight was streaming — just a small square, but enough to show Him to me. Seated on the hard floor with hands tied in front, with spittle on His face and beard, which He can do nothing to remove, His back a little relieved by leaning against the wall behind Him — "Omnipotence in Bonds," to quote Newman's phrase from another context. The stigma of the jail was upon Him.

This is the spectacle that presents itself to Mary at the street corner on the following day. He moves slowly into view, falls heavily to the ground, drags Himself somehow to His feet again, forces His eyes open, weighed down as they are with blood and spittle, and finds Himself looking straight into the eyes of His mother. Mother though she is, she can scarcely recognize Him. The devastating hands of sin have been at work upon Him, and under their action He has become, as it were, a leper. "Who can understand sin?" asks the psalmist. Only those who kneel here with Mary and see sin portrayed in its true colors.

Keyword: STIGMA

Third Section

This meeting may be regarded as the offertory of the Mass soon to be celebrated on Calvary. Jesus and Mary might well have used the prayer from our own liturgy: "We come to you, Father, with praise and thanksgiving . . . We ask you to accept and bless these gifts we offer you in sacrifice. . . ." Mary, in obscurity for many years, appeared now at this tragic moment. Her mother's heart told her what to do. Christ was human as well as divine, and her presence would make the stony road a little less painful and the final struggle a little less terrible.

We want her at the consummation of our sacrifice too, "now and at the hour of *our* death." Says Newman: "O my Lord and my Savior, support me in my last hour by the strong arms of Thy sacraments. Let Thy absolving words be said over me and Thy holy oil seal me. Let Thy own body be my food and Thy blood my sprinkling, and let Thy Mother Mary come to me. . . . May He support us all the day long, till the shadows lengthen, and the evening comes, and the busy world is hushed, and the fever of life is o'er and our work is done. . . ."

Keyword: HOUR OF OUR DEATH

FIFTH STATION:
SIMON

Setting: A crisis is imminent. The centurion on horseback looks critically at each of the three prisoners. The two stalwart brigands do not worry him, but about Jesus he has serious doubts. Although He was not as robust as the other two, He has had much harsher treatment. He must have help if He is not to die on their hands. But where? No Jew would contaminate himself by touching the cross, and no foreigner would volunteer to assist a despised Jew. Most opportunely at this moment a stranger appears, Simon of Cyrene. Two soldiers are ordered to seize him by the shoulders and force him into position behind Christ. He protests violently, but they will not take no for an answer.

First Section

Simon was to receive a grace that would transform his life. He came casually into the city that morning with his two boys, Alexander and Rufus. They had probably been working on a plot outside the northern wall. They were peckish after their hours in the early morning and needing no one to remind them that it was dinnertime. Simon, in his wildest dreams, could never have imagined what was going to happen. He walked onto the stage to perform one single scene in the drama, after which he disappears and is never heard of again.

That one scene has been put on record by three evangelists. Because of it his name will live when the names of kings and sages and builders of nations will have been long forgotten. The suggestion that he should do this infuriated Simon. A self-

respecting man like himself to be associated with this contemptible creature clothed in rags, covered with blood and spattered
with mud! He had to be bullied into doing what was asked of
him. Artists generally represent Simon holding up the foot of the
cross so that it no longer trails along the ground. But the relief
given to Jesus thus would have been almost negligible. It seems
more likely that they both shared the heavier end between them
or even that Simon carried it alone. In the third station we saw
three attitudes towards the cross — rejection, resignation, and
acceptance. Simon passed through all three.

Keyword: MY YOKE

Second Section

Jesus needed help only because He willed to need it. There is
something extraordinarily moving in the fact that He turns to ask
cooperation from one of His creatures. To be employed by Him
to lift up out of sin the souls of others, to inspire those living a
good life to aim at high sanctity — this, when we reflect on it,
must be seen as an unspeakable privilege. But it is also a weighty
obligation. Pope Pius XII insists that "it is a subject of inexhaustible meditation" that other souls may depend, even for their eternal salvation, on how each one of us fulfills our apostolate. We
have not received the gift of the true faith for ourselves alone.
The servant in the parable who buried his talent and handed it
back just as he had received it, was stigmatized as "wicked and
slothful."

Keyword: COOPERATION

Third Section

Simon seems to have been a plain unassuming man, living con-
tentedly with his wife and family. His action throws emphasis,

therefore, on the privilege and obligation of the apostolate of the laity. His two sons were well known and honored by the early Church. St. Paul counted them among his special friends, calling Rufus, in his letter to the Romans, his "chosen friend in the Lord." He greeted the mother too, asserting that she had been also a mother to himself.

Simon stands at the head of a long line of followers who, for two thousand years, have been helping Christ to carry His cross. We may think of him as the acolyte chosen to serve the Mass of the high priest on Calvary.

Keyword: POPE PIUS XII

SIXTH STATION:
VERONICA

Setting: Veronica is watching the procession, perhaps from a window in her house. Christ moves into the picture sadly disfigured, utterly spent. With that instinctive sympathy that is one of God's many beautiful gifts to woman, she asks herself what she can do about it. She steps out into the street, elbows her way through soldiers and mob, till she is quite close to the prisoner. Then she pulls the veil off her head and with it wipes away some of the sweat and blood. She would have wished to do more, but the rasping voice of the centurion barks out an order to have her removed at once. Indeed she would not have succeeded in giving even this slight relief to Christ except that her sudden, impulsive action had taken them all completely by surprise.

First Section

There is, first, the *thoughtfulness* of Veronica's deed. The amount of relief was small, but the gesture itself had an intrinsic value. It was proof to the poor sufferer that somebody cared. There were scores of people milling around Him. Not all of them were hostile, but, seemingly, the thought just did not occur to them that this was a case where something ought to be done. Lack of thoughtfulness accounts largely for the failure of Dives to help Lazarus — who, we suggest, lying in his rags and sores, bears a striking resemblance to Christ in this station. In his case there was no Veronica.

Thoughtfulness, if it was widespread, would fill this dark world with light. You read of the tragic death of a young man you did not know; his parents get a letter of sympathy from you in tomorrow's mail. You phone your congratulations to the student who has done brilliantly; at the railway you offer to carry the bag under which the girl is staggering; you drop into hospital tonight to see how John is after the operation he had at ten this morning.

We saw Simon helping Christ and now we have Veronica's gracious gesture. Our world is calling out for more Simons, more Veronicas, to show thoughtfulness for Christ in His members.

Keyword: THOUGHTFULNESS

Second Section

Veronica needed *courage*. The surmise is that she was a young girl in her twenties. The bodyguard accompanying Christ might well have resented the intrusion of this meddlesome damsel. She could have been injured physically. Her appearance might have provoked some lewd jests and insulting insinuations. But Veronica was a strong character whose determination and independence made them ashamed of themselves. She ignored their very existence. She wanted Christ, and no power on earth or in hell was going to hold her back from Him. She had physical courage; she was also enriched with a fund of moral courage that nothing could thwart.

Could we regard St. Maria Goretti as her modern counterpart? She had the courage to let herself be hacked to pieces rather than yield to the evil suggestions of the man who was infatuated by her. And she was barely twelve, and she is of our own day. Many of us who are good enough would be somewhere near the saints only for the cankerworm of human respect.

Keyword: COURAGE

Third Section

Christ accepted relief. He let Simon help Him, and He gratefully allowed Veronica to wipe His face. Hoffman shows her opening out her veil for Our Lady and Magdalene and John to see. There is the imprint of the face of Christ, standing for all time as God's way of saying thank you. Ingratitude stung His sensitive heart. He cured ten lepers and complained when only one returned to thank Him. He sat on the brow of a hill and wept over the city of Jerusalem because of its ingratitude.

Gratitude expresses itself not in words only. It is suspect if our words do not translate themselves into deeds.

Keyword: GRATITUDE

SEVENTH STATION:
SECOND FALL

Setting: Father Stephen Curran, Jesuit, was taken to hospital for a very serious operation. After more than two hours on the table he was brought back to his bed, hovering between life and death. Gradually he began to gather a little strength, and a flicker of hope stirred in his heart. But we, his friends, knew that the first operation was only a preparation for a much more critical and painful one. The news was broken to him as tactfully as possible, but it nearly broke him. He admitted to me that the prospect terrified him. I met the surgeon on his way out after operation two. "He's alive, poor man," he told me, "but you'll have to pray for him." He died that night.

First Section

Perhaps Christ can walk a little less painfully now that Simon is sharing the weight of the cross with Him. Perhaps He can see His way a little more clearly now that Veronica has cleansed His face. But we can never allow ourselves to forget, as St. John tells us, that He knew everything that was about to befall Him. So He realized that this slight alleviation was only a temporary respite. Unlike Father Curran, He was perfectly well aware that a second ordeal was pending. He stumbled over a large stone and fell heavily, with the full weight of the cross upon Him. We may assume that Simon lifted it and Him at once, but not before this second fall had taken its toll.

Shall we meet our Simon in the Christlike priest who advises and absolves? In the friend who is willing to listen when we want somebody with whom to share our sorrow? It may be a tangled skein, and maybe he cannot find the solution, but we know he is genuinely concerned and praying for us.

Veronica may come into a young man's life in the person of a noble-hearted girl with strength of character whom he learns to reverence and love and recognize as the one chosen for him by God to be his life-partner. Veronica may be a dedicated nursing nun, a missionary, a contemplative, living selflessly in a leper settlement or hidden with Christ in the desert. They are to be found in every walk of life, the Simons and the Veronicas of today.

After a little consolation Christ falls again. Our lives, too, alternate between consolation and sorrow. These complement each other. Life on earth is a time of testing.

Second Section

There was a first fall for Jesus and a last fall, and the falls in between. When St. Francis learned that one of his brethren had come to grief by pride he prostrated himself on the ground and remained there a considerable time saying: "Only here is a man safe." We cannot fall off the ground.

Whether we are aiming at high holiness or trying to break off a habit of serious sin, our falls teach us the absolute need of God's grace. "Without me you can do nothing." A chastening thought. If we have learned through our falls how weak and inconstant we are, they will have helped to lay the only solid foundation on which to build a spiritual life. Pride, self-sufficiency, hard and scornful, disappears and gives way to a tolerance modeled on the command of Him who told us forgive till seventy times seven times.

Our falls school us thus in humility. They also make our hearts overflow with gratitude to God; His patience with us gives us some insight into the greatness of the love He has for us. If without Him we can do nothing, St. Paul fills us with courage to get up after each fall by assuring us that we can do "all things in Him Who strengthens us."

Satan offers us pleasure, which will certainly be followed by remorse. Christ puts to us a sacrifice, which will inevitably bring us immense peace of soul.

Keyword: OUR FALLS

EIGHTH STATION:
WEEPING WOMEN

Setting: In the missal as we used to have it there was a prayer for the gift of tears. "Lord, draw from our stony hearts tears of compunction that we may be able to mourn for our sins and win forgiveness for them...." We are inclined to associate tears with women more than with men. We may even have a lurking suspicion that tears in a man indicate a lack of manhood. But Christ shed tears at the grave of His friend Lazarus and when He looked down from Olivet on ungrateful Jerusalem. The subject matter of this eighth station is the tears of the women who wept for Jesus.

First Section

Jesus accepted the help given Him by Simon and the gracious sympathy of Veronica. But in this station He tells these good women to dry their tears or, if weep they must, let their mourning be not for Him. There is no suggestion of harshness in His way of saying this, no sign of displeasure or annoyance. He is teaching them, rather, and us through them, that there are times when we are to abstain from creaturely consolations. "Let each one reflect," writes St. Ignatius, "that he will advance in all spiritual things in the measure in which he rids himself of self-love, of doing his own will, of consulting his own convenience."

There was none of this selfishness needing purification in Christ, but His reaction, to Simon and Veronica on the one hand and to the weeping women on the other, is highly instructive. There is a time for accepting gratefully from God's hand things which are naturally pleasant, and there is a time when they should be sacrificed in a spirit of loving detachment.

Much sincerity is necessary, and much divine enlightenment, in order to see when to take and when to go without. To yield habitually is to cultivate the cult of softness. To insist rigidly always on choosing what is hard might easily turn us into Manicheans. We need careful guidance here from our spiritual director.

Keyword: "WEEP NOT"

Second Section

"Weep not over me but over yourselves and your children." He foresees the complete destruction of Jerusalem with all the carnage and bloodshed and famine. The hated Romans would mow them down, men, women and children — some of whom were standing beside Him today.

There is a clear echo of these words in our day. "Every year," writes Alan Hart, "fifteen million children under five die of malnutrition — not hunger, not starvation, but that day-in-day-out erosion of health through lack of adequate food. ... There are already three hundred million children in the Third World, physically and mentally retarded." Father Paul Crane, S.J., in a public lecture, deplored our apathy in the West for this appalling state of affairs and I find the same bitter complaint in Hart's article.

It is not that we have been left without warning. God has sent His Mother many times in these years to insist on the vital need of prayer and penance. Many people, thank God, are doing their utmost to implement the instructions of Our Lady. But for too many of us they fall on deaf ears. Even priests and religious are often not interested, pretend to discredit the messages, wanting only not to be disturbed. With good reason does Christ tell us to weep over our children and the future ahead of them.

Keyword: YOUR CHILDREN

Third Section

"Prophets of Doom." It might be fairly argued that this phrase, generally used in a deprecatory sense, might be applied to Jesus and Mary. We have only to recall the warnings of Christ to the pharisees and their frightening relevance to the Church and world today. This is not pessimism but to live with our feet on the ground.

Keyword: PROPHETS OF DOOM?

NINTH STATION:
THIRD FALL

Setting: Christ's address to the weeping women shows Him completely in control of the situation throughout the Passion. He halts here because He wants to halt. He speaks unhurriedly although He is well aware of the impatience of His enemies to reach Calvary and see Him die. Quite firmly He imposes a delay, and they feel powerless to oppose Him. He stops dead and delivers His message at His own pace, the significance increased by the dignified and authoritative manner in which it is spoken. When He was quite finished they try to make up for lost time by urging Him forward all the more. Perhaps this extra pressure put on Him accounts for His third fall, which took place only a few yards from the altar of sacrifice.

First Section

It is not fantastic to regard this final fall as a gesture of reverence. Christ stands in front of the altar where He is about to say Mass, and He first prostrates Himself in humble adoration. This is the holiest sanctuary on earth. No wonder, then, that the priest begins His Mass with a profound genuflection. Dr. Orchard, not yet a Catholic, attended Mass in a Paris church. As they came out he said to his companion: "I don't know whether Catholics are right or wrong in what they believe about the Mass. But this much I will say — that priest we have just seen at the altar believes in what he is doing."

As I type these lines there arises before my eyes the image of Brother Clement, the sacristan in charge of the Redemptorist

Church in Limerick. Many a time as a small boy did I watch him genuflecting before the Blessed Sacrament. He was old and stooped and walked with difficulty. But every time he passed in front of the tabernacle he insisted on bending his knee till it touched the ground. The effort obviously cost him much, but never would he let himself off. That genuflection was a constant sermon, relevant still.

Keyword: REVERENCE

Second Section

The enemies of Christ were restless. Goaded by passion, they must be shouting, issuing orders, bullying their underlings, trembling with excitement, devoid of self-control. They are like that today too. Communism aims at getting control of men's thinking, constantly preoccupied with one scheme after another. This stage of agitation prevents them from examining dispassionately and calmly the goal to which they are being guided. They are always in a hurry.

What a contrast to this do we find when we look into the heart of Christ! Here there is immense peace and self-possession and serenity. What is the secret? It is that face-to-face vision of God, which He never lost for a moment. He can retire into Himself and ignore, in large measure, the tumult round about Him outside. He tells us do the same. "Let not your heart be troubled. You believe in God; believe also in me." In His presence our restless agitation is quieted. Our problems, if not solved, are seen in a new perspective. In the depths of our own souls there is waiting for us the peace of God surpassing all understanding.

Keyword: AGITATION

Third Section

"Permit not that I ever offend Thee again." In this prayer we ask that as Christ reached His last fall, so we may have reached ours. The prodigal son kept falling till he finally found himself in the misery and squalor of the pigsty. It was only then that he said, "I will arise and go back to my father." It was his last fall. Matt Talbot, a slave to drink, encountered a mighty grace, in the strength of which he began to walk the way of the saints. We are now permitted to hope for his canonization. "Put your sins under your feet," advises St. Augustine, "and they will lift you all the higher up to God." There MUST be a last fall; why not now?

Keyword: MY LAST FALL

TENTH STATION:
JESUS STRIPPED

Setting: St. Paul reminds the Philippians that Christ "emptied himself, taking the form of a servant." Though He remained always God He renounced the exterior signs by which His divinity could be recognized. Isaiah saw Him as "truly a hidden God ... the savior ... without beauty, without majesty ... despised and rejected by men." His self-emptying is first seen when He subjects Himself to the laws of human birth and growth and to the lowliness of our human nature. It is symbolized here in this tenth station. The laying aside of His garments is a reminder of the laying aside of His divinity by becoming a man like us; throughout the Passion especially, "the divinity hides itself," as St. Ignatius would have us note carefully.

First Section

Communism has taken over many of our Christian ideals, has rebaptized them and distorted them in the process. It has found the secret of inspiring its votaries with a zeal and enthusiasm comparable to what we find in St. Paul or St. Francis Xavier. "More emphatically than similar movements in the past," writes Pope Pius XI, "it conceals within itself a false messianic idea. A pseudo-ideal of justice, of equality, of fraternity, impregnates all its doctrines and activity with a deceptive mysticism, which communicates a zealous and contagious enthusiasm. . . ."

The response it evokes is a challenge to us Catholics and an indictment. Communism demands everything, total dedication. We are timid about asking too much from those whom we profess to be leading to close following of Christ. There is no challenge in the watered-down version of His teaching as we present it to them. Christ "emptied Himself," even to the lengths of taking the clothes off His back.

Father Dan Lord writes about priests who used to come to his school looking for vocations. If they painted a rosy picture, describing the comforts possible to have in the priesthood, they drew a blank. It was the priest who preached Christ and Him crucified who attracted them. Cardinal Paul Leger, who has laid aside his purple to live as a missionary among lepers, writes: "Here, at any rate, I feel I can talk about poverty without being too much of a hypocrite."

Keyword: CHALLENGE

Second Section

St. Paul tells the Romans: "Put on the Lord Jesus Christ and make not provision for the flesh in its concupiscences." Self-emptying is vitally important. But laying aside the garments is only the negative part of our task. Positively, we must "put on Christ." To understand what this means we turn to the fifteenth chapter of St. John's gospel. When we have read it, we read it again and again. It is inexhaustible. Here is part of the sublime ideal traced for us by Christ Himself: "Make your home in me and I in you. . . . As the Father has loved me, so have I loved you. Abide in my love. If you keep my commandments you will abide in my love . . . I have told you this that my joy may be in you and that your joy may be filled."

These are stunning words describing Christ's design in asking us to empty ourselves. When our hearts are empty He fills them with Himself. And note how often He used the word "abide," to show us His meaning. This divine indwelling is not a passing visit from Him to the soul. It is permanent. It begins here on earth to be perfected in heaven. Here it is like the first glint of light in the eastern sky at dawn; there it will be the sun bursting into full splendor at noonday.

Keyword: ABIDE

Third Section

This is all magnificently illustrated in the story of Edel Quinn, Legion of Mary envoy to Africa. I hope you have *NOT* read it because of the treat in store for you. "Her utter selflessness and entire and confiding abandonment to God were never at fault . . . "A fascinating exterior hid an incredible strength."

Keyword: EDEL

ELEVENTH STATION:
NAILED TO THE CROSS

Setting: Our Lord was probably first tied to the cross before being nailed. Otherwise the nervous twitch would have ripped open the hands and feet. It is likely, too, that He was tied like this to an erect cross already planted firmly in the solid ground. So His executioners would have first stretched out each arm full along the transverse beam, making both secure with several coils of rope or cord. Then each leg was treated similarly. How agonizing the pain was must be left to our imagination. For even a strong man in perfect health this would be torture. What, then, must it have been for Christ in view of all He suffered since He was taken in the garden last night?

First Section
In Exodus 17 Moses knelt in prayer on the top of a hill, praying for his people who had been attacked by the Amelikites in the valley below. As long as he kept his arms extended Israel had the advantage, but when they began to droop the tide turned and danger threatened. So Aaron and Hur supported them. Jesus' arms do not droop now. They are kept in position by two nails. If the prayer of Moses was so effective, what may we not expect from His prayer? Moses was a servant, but Jesus is the well-beloved Son. Such a prayer, offered by such a person and in such circumstances, is certain to call down immense graces on us.

"God sent fiery serpents among the people, and their bite brought death to many" (Numbers 21:6). The people repented. God forgave them. He ordered Moses to set up a brazen serpent, and He promised healing to all who looked upon it. The parallel between this and Calvary is easy to see. We sinners have no mere brazen serpent to look upon with sorrow and confidence. Satan may have injected the poison of sin into our souls, but what a remedy has God provided for our complete healing!

"If I be lifted up from the earth," said Christ, "I will draw all men to myself" (John 12:32). It is now no longer a mere cleansing from sin, but a tasting and a seeing that the Lord is sweet.

Keyword: SERPENTS

Second Section

Christ forgives. Christ invites us to close friendship with Himself. When the truth of this begins to dawn in our dull minds; when we glimpse the vast chasm between our own utter insignificance and the power and beauty and knowledge of God; and when we reflect that God, being Who He is, permits us to love Him and even begs us to love; when all this becomes living reality, we must be almost crushed by the weight of such truth. The saints do not exaggerate. They are simply grappling with words to tell us what they know by personal experience. No words are forceful enough, luminous enough. The saints, who have penetrated somewhat into the truth of this eleventh station, can hardly suppress a feeling of holy impatience at the sight of our apathy, and of sadness because they know what we are missing. Life becomes a competition in the art of giving, They give to Christ, and He is the other competitor. The other competitor wins every time.

Keyword: NO EXAGGERATION

Third Section

The soldiers offered Christ a drink, but "when he had tasted, he would not drink" (Matthew 27:34). The drink might have deadened the fearful pain and eased His parched thirst, he refused it in the same spirit as He brushed aside the tears of the women He had met on His way to this place. He had asked the woman at the well for a drink of water, but He had begged His Father not to insist that He should drink the chalice. There are times when He is prepared to accept and times when He refuses. We have seen why in the eighth station.

Keyword: THE OTHER COMPETITOR

TWELFTH STATION:
JESUS DIES

Setting: Christ died for us sinners. We do not want to forget, but rather to remember with gratitude and joy, that many sinners died for Christ. Nor is martyrdom for any one of us the mere remote possibility it used to be. There are two significant details about Christ's last moments. First, He cried out with a strong, loud voice, just before the end. No mere man could have done that in view of what Christ had suffered. It was proof that He was God. It drew from the centurion a magnificent act of faith. "The centurion, who was standing in front of him, had seen how he had died and he said: 'In truth this man was the Son of God'" (Mark 15:39). We read also that, "bowing down His head, he gave up the ghost" (John 19:30). This gesture suggests that He is giving permission to death to come for Him.

First Section

A street artist exhibited five or six pictures for the passers-by to see. He headed the selection with a caption in large letters: "All my own work." As I stand watching the dying Christ and reflect on what He has suffered, must I say that this is "all my own work"? Must I class myself with those who "were once brought into the light and tasted the gift of heaven and received a share of the Holy Spirit and appreciated the good message of God and the powers of the world to come and yet, in spite of this, have fallen away . . . and wilfully crucified the Son of God and openly mocked Him"? God forbid! But salutary fear is wholesome. I have no guarantee that I shall persevere. I have to work out my salvation "in fear and trembling." But this very uncertainty must be balanced by immense confidence. When we go to Mass, which is the prolongation of the Passion, we say: "Though we are sinners, we trust in Your mercy and love." If, as I contemplate this twelfth station, I find it still possible to deny, or even doubt, "the height and depth and length and breadth" of that love and mercy, then an omnipotent lover has taxed the powers of His omnipotence in vain.

Keyword: MY OWN WORK

Second Section

It is helpful to pause and listen here. Calvary was near a city gate, situated between two important roads, one going to Jaffa and the other to Damascus. People passed up and down continually. They taunted Him. "Ha! You boasted you could destroy God's temple. . . . Now, then, save yourself." Some of the Jewish leaders were here too, gloating over their victory. Even His two fellow criminals upbraided Him, though one of them was won over to His side. He reflected on the appalling sufferings Christ had endured during the three hours since they left the city. Throughout, not a suggestion of anger, not a single gesture of impatience, not a syllable of complaint had escaped Him. Jesus is no mere man.

Mary listens with us. She hears what we have been hearing. She has noted the marvelous silence of Jesus. She listens to the coarse language of the soldiers, seated and playing dice, their job done, filling in time till the three criminals die. She hears them haggling over the coat of her Son and finally deciding to cast lots for it. What would she not have given to lay hands on it and bring it home!

Christ's own voice was heard here too, but what He said

we shall learn on another page. Prayer is a listening as well as a speaking.

Keyword: LISTENING

Third Section

The ceiling in the Sistine Chapel is one of Michelangelo's masterpieces. But what a price he paid for it, lying flat on his back for three years with paint dropping on his face and his sight so impaired that ever after when he wanted to read he had to hold the book above his head. Suppose that under cover of night an enemy of his had wrecked his work, hacking at the ceiling and blotting out those exquisite images. This is a feeble illustration of what is done in the soul, Christ's masterpiece, by sin. All my own work!

Keyword: MICHELANGELO

THIRTEENTH STATION:
DESCENT FROM THE CROSS

Setting: Christ's enemies, on Good Friday and still today, try to discredit the fact of His death on the cross. But we are clearly told that Joseph of Arimathea and Nicodemus went to Pilate and boldly demanded permission to take down Christ's body and bury it. Pilate was surprised to hear that Jesus was already dead, so he called for an inquiry and got an official statement testifying to the death. He also gave the necessary permission for the burial. Further, we know that a soldier came to each of the three crosses to break the legs of the criminals and did not break the legs of Christ because he saw that "he was already dead." When Jesus actually rose from the grave the pharisees gave money to the guards telling them to say that while they were asleep the body of Christ had been stolen!

First Section

Joseph and Nicodemus had been attracted by Jesus, but they were inclined to hide the fact for fear of the Jews. It is heartening for us to see how their courage has grown. They *demanded* the body, and *boldly*. It is said that Joseph suffered imprisonment and death at the hands of the pharisees for his interference.

They place the ladders close to the cross and hammer the nails out of the hands of Christ. The back of each hand is stuck to the beam, held there by congealed blood. The arms, dislocated, do not fall into their natural position but remain still extended. One of the men supports the body while the other takes the nails out of the feet. Only now has Christ accepted the challenge to come down from the cross.

His mother sits there and takes Him onto her lap. Michelangelo has immortalized the scene in his "canticle in stone." "The limp body, flexed, so that it reposes upon the virgin's lap, has all the serenity of death; only the pierced hands and side denote Christ's agony. With slightly inclined head the mother gazes tenderly upon her Son. On her face there is an expression of interior sorrow and mute acceptance of the divine will." There is joy as well as sorrow here. Our Lord told Juliana of Norwich: "Suddenly you will be taken from all your pain, all your sickness, all your discomfort. You will come up above, with Me as your reward. . . . Never again will there be any sort of suffering or unhappiness. . . . Why should it grieve you to suffer a little while, seeing that this is My will and My glory?" The body is now carried over to "the stone of unction" — a large flat slab of marble, convenient for embalming. Some horsemen, riding past, seeing the ghastly appearance of the dead man, ask what crimes had He committed. The answer is that He did all things well.

Keyword: STONE OF UNCTION

Second Section

Sorrowing mothers today shed tears for the young son killed in a bomb explosion. There is grief for the boy who is mentally handicapped. Mothers worry when Jim or Tom in faraway India has not written for over a year; when their boy refuses to go to Mass or maybe ridicules the practice of confession. All such mothers should often kneel or sit with Mary in this thirteenth station. She knows. She understands.

Note, too, that neither Christ nor His mother bore any resentment for those who made them suffer. Indeed Jesus prayed for them. Mamma Assunta, mother of St. Maria Goretti, willingly forgave the murderer of her daughter, whom he had tried in vain to seduce to sin.

Keyword: MOTHERS TODAY

Third Section

Mothers can foster vocations. The Curé of Ars used to say: "To my mother I owe all the love of God and souls I have. One memory I have; she always came herself to waken us in the morning, so as to make sure that the moment we opened our eyes we lifted up our hearts to God in prayer."

Keyword: CURE OF ARS

FOURTEENTH STATION:
THE FUNERAL

Setting: Jesus was born in the poverty of a stable. In backwater Nazareth He had little of this world's goods. During the three years of public life He did not have a place to lay His head. Now comes His funeral. It is understatement to say there was no pomp or ceremonial. Rather, it was a sorry little part of "nobodies," following the remains of a criminal who had died in disgrace. Nicodemus and Joseph came along providentially and undertook to find a burial place and defray the expenses of the funeral. They thus saved Our Lady from deep embarrassment, for it seems probable that she could have contributed little or nothing, in which case Jesus would have been given a pauper's grave.

First Section

By what seems a paradox, Christ died a poor man and yet left immense wealth behind Him. His last will and testament is an amazing document. When it is opened and read we learn that every person coming into this world is presented with a blank check and told to fill it in for whatever amount he wishes! When a rich man dies there is often a dispute about his will because no matter how much he left, there is a limit. But Christ left infinite wealth; you can take from infinity as much as ever you wish, and infinity remains. Christ's riches do not consist of tawdry gold and silver, which death snatches from us. They are not lost at death, but rather, their possession is guaranteed forever.

Material wealth is not necessarily an obstacle to sanctity. But the abundance of Christ's riches is discovered oftener in the mud cabin than in the house of the rich man. Sanctity is a delicate flower, needing an especially congenial atmosphere for its growth. Actual poverty, or that spirit of poverty we call detachment, provides the atmosphere.

That is why Christ deliberately preferred to be poor; why He blessed the poor in spirit; why He told the rich young man to get rid of his money if he wanted to be perfect; why He warned in such emphatic language that riches are a danger and a snare. I often think of the complete transformation happening when the "nobodies" enter into the everlasting inheritance.

Keyword: NOBODIES

Second Section

There is joy mixed with the sorrows of Good Friday. There is lavish wealth being distributed by the poor man who left infinite treasure. There is joy in Limbo when, after thousands of years, Christ at last comes to deliver the souls waiting there. Adam, who sinned, sees this second Adam who has come to take away the sins of the world. The prophets and patriarchs of the Old Law; the wonderful women who lived before Christ; Elizabeth and Zechariah and their son John; St. Joseph, foster-father of Jesus — all these and many others come to mind as we enter that prisonhouse in spirit with the risen Christ.

When St. Paul thought along these lines he found Himself torn between two desires. He craved for the day when the dream would come true, desiring "to be dissolved and be with Christ." But there was also the truth that while he remained on earth he could toil for souls and distribute among them the riches of Christ. St. Ignatius was asked what his choice would be if he was told he might die at once, with a guarantee that he would save his soul, or continue living without that assurance. He answered without hesitation that he would go on living.

Keyword: JOY ON GOOD FRIDAY

Third Section

How did Lazarus and the son of the widow of Naim adjust
themselves to this world after they had died and returned? How
would Hitler, Stalin or Mao shape their lives if they were back
again? What would Howard Hughes do with his millions? One
sometimes thinks that we are rather like ants on an anthill!
"Only one thing is necessary." That we shall see very clearly at
the hour of death. Why not now?

Keyword: NO RETURN

FIFTEENTH STATION:
JESUS RISES AGAIN

Setting: Christ said He would rise from the dead. "Destroy this temple," He told the Jews, "and in three days I will rebuild it." But He spoke of the temple that was His body. Some deliberately misinterpreted Him, pretending to think that He meant the material temple in which they stood. They showed their hand when, after Calvary, they asked Pilate to place a guard at the tomb "because we have remembered that the seducer said . . . he would rise again." Our Lord predicted several times to His apostles that He would rise again. On several occasions He described the terrible program of suffering awaiting Him, but invariably He added: "On the third day the Son of Man will rise again." The Resurrection is the supreme proof of the divinity of Christ. Take away the Resurrection and the whole superstructure of the Catholic faith falls to the ground. The enemies of the faith know this well; hence in every age they have labored to disprove the Resurrection.

First Section

The patience of Job has passed into a proverb. He lost his children and his extensive property. A loathsome disease broke out in his body, and the poor man sat on a dungheap and scraped away the sores with a potsherd. His wife came out and reproached him bitterly. His so-called friends clearly intimated that he must be a great sinner. How did he refrain from anger? Largely by his belief in a future resurrection. "I know that my redeemer lives and that in the last day I shall rise . . . and in my flesh I shall see my God. ... This, my hope, is laid up in my bosom."

Like Job we are all expected to live in the resurrection spirit. Newman writes: "Do you know the feeling in matters of this life, of expecting a friend, expecting him to come and he delays? Do you know what it is to be in unpleasant company, and to wish for the time to pass away, and the hour strike when you may be set at liberty? Do you know what it is to be in anxiety lest something should happen, which may happen or may not, or to be in suspense about some important event, which makes your heart beat as often as you are reminded of it? ... What it is to live upon a person who is present with you, that your eyes follow him, that you read his soul, that you see all the changes in his countenance?

"To watch for Christ is a feeling such as all these. ... He watches for Christ who has a sensitive, eager, comprehensive mind: who is awake, alive, quick-sighted, zealous in seeking and honoring Him: who looks out for Him in all that happens, and who would not be surprised, who would not be over-agitated or overwhelmed if he found that He was coming at once?" (*Parochial and Plain Sermons:* "Watching," Vol IV). This is what is meant by living in the spirit of the Resurrection.

Keyword: JOB

Second Section

St. Thomas gives five reasons why the Resurrection was necessary. First, God's justice demanded it. It is the fruit and the reward of Christ's perfect humility. "He who humbles himself shall be exalted." Like Him, we are being tested here. We have foes within and enemies without. We grow weary in the day-to-day struggle. We face each new day, perhaps, with a heavy heart. But a just God will restore the balance. "They who sow in tears shall reap in joy."

Secondly, as we have seen, the Resurrection is the foundation of our faith. "My just man lives by faith." The Resurrection is also our hope, without which this world is a blind alley. "If in this world only we have hope in Christ, we are of all men the most miserable" (Romans 15:19). The Resurrection of Christ is our model. Like Him it teaches us to cultivate a taste for divine things and to restrain ourselves from undue attachment to the things of earth. Lastly, our resurrection will put the finishing touches to the work of our redemption. The Passion is negative; it destroys sin. The Resurrection is positive, the infusing of a new life. It marks the crowning of the undertaking. It is the passage from grace to glory. There must be music in every heart which reflects on these truths. We pray: "That Thou wouldst lift up our minds to heavenly desires, we beseech Thee, Lord, to hear us."

Keyword: MUSIC

Third Section

During the forty days between Christ's Resurrection and Ascension we find five relationships He established with His apostles. First, they *saw* Him. They were thunderstruck with amazement when He suddenly showed Himself to them alive, in the upper room in Jerusalem. They could not believe their eyes. It seemed too good to be true. Between my own resurrection now and my ascension into heaven at death, I too must *see* Him with the eye of faith in every circumstance of life.

Since they experienced difficulty in believing because of the sight of Him, He invited them to *touch* Him. He was no ghost, as they suspected, but "only Jesus" with whom they had been on terms of such loving intimacy. Can *we* touch Him too? Mother Teresa of Calcutta lays down for her novices the following principle: "The priest touches the Body of Christ in the Eucharist; we touch Him in the members of His Mystical Body." All her spiritual training is summarized in this. No wonder the response is inspiring.

Jesus, after the Resurrection, *ate and drank* with His friends; indeed He invited Himself to share their meal in the upper room. We are to eat His body and drink His blood in the Eucharist. But St. Paul adds that whenever we eat or drink, or do anything else, we are to share it all with Him.

During those forty days they *spoke* to Him and He to them. We need not envy them their privilege, for prayer is conversation with God. St. Augustine defines it as "the aspiration of the creature and the inspiration of the Creator."

Finally, they spoke *about* Him. We cannot but speak about what we have seen and heard. If our words are seasoned with prayer and sacrifice they are sure to help in bringing Christ back.

Keyword: RELATIONSHIPS

THE LIVING VOICE

FIRST WORD: "Father, Forgive Them: They Know Not What They Do."

We begin this section with a ghastly story. A young man was condemned to be hanged. Before he put his foot on the trapdoor he turned to the priest by his side: "Father," he said, "I have a last request to make. Do your best to find where my mother is and tell her I died cursing her. If she had done her duty by me I would not be here today." Two or three minutes later and he was standing before God to be judged.

That poor man died with a curse on his lips. We read that men condemned to die on a cross often poured out a frightful volley of blasphemy and obscenity, calling down vengeance on those who made them suffer. The soldiers took little notice of this on Calvary. It always happened. But what must have caused them astonishment was that Christ, all through His frightful tortures, had not uttered a syllable of complaint or shown the smallest sign of anger. In all their grim experience they had never before encountered a criminal who behaved like this one.

He was silent while they hammered the nails into His hands and feet, silent when they stretched out His limbs on the cross, silent when it sank with a thud into the ground increasing His agony. Now the cross is in position. Their job is done. All they have still to do is stay around till the three criminals die.

They must have wondered vaguely how the strange man in the center would conduct himself at this stage. The other two had long since begun mouthing their abominations, screaming their invective. But Jesus has preserved His inviolable silence. They squatted on the ground and, to kill time, started to play what we would call a game of cards.

But their attention is suddenly diverted. Jesus, at last, is saying something. Is He, too, now about to contribute His share to the execrations of the other two? If His silence amazed them, what He says now stuns them. Christ maintains a unique role. "Father," He says, "forgive them; they do not know what they are doing." The soldiers and all who heard what He said are incredulous. As though to convince them, Jesus repeated this first word several times.

Go Slow

We often talk about Christ Who *died* on the cross. It is most helpful to reflect that He also lived on the cross, lived there for three hours, using the cross as a pulpit from which to deliver a discourse filled with light. The entire sermon might have been preached in a quarter of an hour. It contained, in all, only seven sentences or "words," but there was a pause after each, and a long break of nearly two hours between the end of the third word and the beginning of the fourth.

This spacing-out was deliberately planned. Jesus is deeply concerned that we do not merely hear but also listen. These words are like seeds sown in the soil of the soul, which must sink in. Otherwise they will be blown away and forgotten. If, like Mary, we ponder them over in our hearts, they may well prove to be the bearer of a grace that will transform our lives.

Forgive

King David committed adultery. He added to his crime by bringing about the death of the woman's innocent husband. God sent the prophet Nathan to rebuke him. Nathan told him about a wealthy man who treated a poor man with shocking injustice and cruelty. David flared up and swore he would punish the offender. But he must have gasped with astonishment at what Nathan said next. "But that evil man, King David, is yourself!" The words went right home. The king recognized himself as the villain of the piece. Humbly and sorrowfully he confessed. "I have sinned against my God," he said. Scarcely had he finished speaking when the prophet assured him that God had forgiven him.

This story is condensed from the first book of Samuel, chapter 12. We cite it to underline the readiness of God to forgive wherever He finds genuine repentance. There was ingratitude in David's sin; there was injustice to the woman's husband; there was scandal, especially in view of his position as king, and, worst of all, the cruel plot to commit murder and the contemptible means employed to cover up his crime. All these sordid details over and above the adultery itself, and at the very first sign of sincere sorrow God hastens to forgive.

A few years ago I read a book named *I Can't Forgive*, written by a man who had managed to survive the horrors of a concentration camp. He has a harrowing description of Hitler arriving one morning to inaugurate the setting-up of a new gas chamber. The unfortunate men were packed in like sardines waiting for him to come and turn on the power and declare the slaughterhouse open. It is very human for the author to say "I Can't Forgive" but inexcusable in the light of Calvary. If we find ourselves hard and vindictive it is chastening to recall our own sins. We too are included in this first word of Christ on the cross.

Father Kolbe

The close similarity between the sufferings of the Franciscan Blessed Maximilian Kolbe and the Passion of Christ is quite startling. He sowed love where he found hatred. A photo shows him standing in the death camp at Auschwitz, worn to a shadow as a result of the inhuman treatment he was given. "Bloody

Krott," ex-criminal and now commandant, hated him because he was a priest, forced him to carry huge tree trunks and run with them. When he fell he was kicked in the stomach and given fifty strokes of the lash. Throughout, like Christ, he preserved unbroken silence. His selflessness reached its climax when he offered to die if a prisoner under sentence was let go free. The offer was accepted. "Greater love than this no man has, that he lay down his life for his friends."

From all this one dynamic lesson emerges. "Let not the sun go down on your anger." "Forgive us our trespasses as we forgive those who trespass against us."

SECOND WORD: "This Day You Shall Be With Me in Paradise"

St. John tells us, in his ninth chapter, the story of a man born blind to whom Jesus gave the gift of sight. Our Lord anointed his eyes with a piece of moistened clay and told him to wash it off in the pool called Siloam. I suppose somebody took the blind man by the hand — perhaps his son or daughter — and guided him to the spot. He was told that he was now standing just at the edge of the pool. He knelt, bent foward slightly and washed off the clay. At that moment, to his inexpressible amazement and joy, he received for the first time in his life the gift of sight.

Sight! Can I not see him kneeling there on the bank with hands joined, staring incredulously and fascinated by everything he sees? On every side he encounters delightful surprises. He lifts up his eyes toward the sun; he had often felt its warmth, but until now he did not have a notion of what it looked like. He gazes in rapture at the white clouds sailing through patches of blue. He never saw color before. Birds are flitting here and there. He marvels at the green grass, the flowers and trees and water; for the first time he sees the face of his son or daughter and the reflection of his own face in the pool. He summed up the story himself in a sentence: "One thing I know, that whereas I was blind, now I see."

Sometimes it is in the mind or heart that this transformation takes place. It is even more astonishing then. We think of Saul of Tarsus, sworn enemy of Christ, riding into Damascus to exterminate His name; seeing a vision, falling from his horse, hearing a voice and rising up a new man. The bigot and persecutor became one of the most zealous apostles of Christ in all history.

History is full of such incidents. They all have one common characteristic. In every case they bring vision, insight, a completely new outlook on the whole of creation. Realization takes over where until now there was mere knowledge. The point is worth illustrating. Everyone knows, for instance, that death is certain, and every Christian at least believes that his lot for all eternity depends on the use he makes of time. This he knows in much the same way as he is aware of the existence of the Sahara. In both cases, very possibly, the knowledge barely grazes the surface of his mind. But one day he stands looking into the open coffin containing the dead body of the mother he loves. It compels him to go down below the surface of things and reflect on them against the background of eternity. Realization and conviction now move in.

Dismas

Sometimes this insight comes only when the person for whom it is intended is near the end of life. This is what happened in the case of Dismas, one of the two thieves between whom Christ was crucified. Little is known of this man's early life. He figures in a legend of which much was made in the first centuries of the Church. It is told that the holy family, fleeing from the sword of Herod into Egypt, was befriended and saved from harm through the intervention of a highwayman, a member of a gang of robbers. The son of their chief undertook to protect the fugitives. He pointed out to his associates that they were quite poor and had no evil intentions. All they wanted was permission to pass through. The others persisted, whereupon the chief's son produced forty drachmas for their ransom.

This was accepted and they were let go. As they left, Mary said to their deliverer: "May God uphold you with His right hand and grant you forgiveness of your sins!" The tradition is that this young man was Dismas. St. Cyril of Jerusalem, St.

Chrysostom and others seem to accept the story. They suggest that this act on the part of the robber chief won him the grace of conversion.

We move now from conjecture and legend into the field of authentic history; into history, in fact, the truth of which is attested by the Holy Spirit Himself in the gospel. What St. Luke has to tell us about the repentant thief can be compressed into a few sentences. But there is precious ore buried in them, the beauty of which can be discovered only when they are exposed fully to the light of day. If we find it we are sure to derive courage and inspiration from our meditation.

It was only when the prodigal son had sunk about as low as was possible that he remembered how genuine was the love of his father. It was only when he found himself seated in the misery and squalor of of the pigsty, herding swine, the unclean animals of the Jews, that he realized his folly and ingratitude. He had flung aside all semblance of self-control, indulging every impulse, trying to persuade himself that happiness lay this way. He was disgusted, disillusioned. Was there anyone left to whom he could turn, who would believe in him still, somebody with an understanding mind and a loving heart? He knew the answer. "I will arise and go back to my father." And we know that his father rushed out to meet him and welcome him home.

Prodigal

The experience of Dismas is very similar. It might be regarded as almost the actual working-out of the parable. He, too, has drunk to the dregs the intoxications of the world and found they left his heart empty. Without his knowing it, as he hangs here on the cross, transformation is close to him. He has witnessed in Christ an unalterable patience, which is more than human. He has heard Him actually praying for the very persons who treated Him so savagely. His own world has collapsed down about his ears. Could it be possible that Christ is the answer? "Lord," he prayed, "remember me when you come into Your kingdom." Everyone else has cast him aside. Nothing is left except the white ashes of a wasted life. Would Christ accept even these?

It is a poor compliment to Christ that Dismas turns to Him only when everyone else has let him down. Would any of us presume to treat a human friend like this? He offers me his friendship and I reject it. I go my own way only to find that I too am unwanted. Years pass and I continue to ignore him. Suppose that it is only after a lifetime, when there is no one else to fall back upon, that I finally show myself willing to accept his friendship. If even now at "five minutes to midnight," when my life has all but run its course, he shows himself still willing and eager to have me, I have surely found a friend whose friendship must be almost unique.

This is the theme of Francis Thompson's immortal poem. All these years the soul has been fleeing from Christ. It is only now that "the Hound of Heaven" is given a chance to overtake its flight: "Whom wilt thou find to love ignoble thee, save Me, save only Me?" As Shakespeare wrote, "The friends thou hast, and their adoption tried, grapple them to thy soul with hoops of steel."

The vastly consoling truth is that Christ accepts Dismas, accepts him eagerly, even at this eleventh hour. The thief had made a modest enough request — a mere "memento" in Christ's Mass. "Lord, remember me. . . ." Jesus responds with divine liberality. Not a remembrance only but: "I solemnly promise you that this day you will be with me in paradise." The only saint canonized before his death; canonized, not by pope or the voice of the people, but in a formula composed by Christ Himself. With joy did *SAINT* Dismas hear it. If regret at that moment were possible for him, it would be in the thought that while he had indeed found Christ, he had made the discovery *only now*.

The Other Thief

At first Dismas had joined with his companion in cursing Christ. "The self-same things the *thieves* who were crucified with him reproached him and reviled him . . . 'If you are the Son of God, save yourself and us.'" To each of the two Christ offered a mighty grace, but the unrepentant thief rejected it. The heart cannot be forced to love; it must be won. Christ offers. Christ appeals. Christ promises. Christ warns and even threatens. But He compels no one. He waited even for Mary to give her free consent to the Incarnation. In assessing the grace offered to the unrepentant thief, we must not restrict ourselves to what we heard Christ say and saw Him do. The profound change in his companion cannot but have impressed him. Dismas had begun by joining in the blasphemies against Christ. Then he lapsed into silence. When next he spoke it was to pray to Christ and rebuke his companion severely. "Have you no fear of God at all?" he asked. "You got the same sentence as he did, but in our case we deserved it: we are paying for what we did. But this man has done no evil." Here is humble confession of his sins; an effort to convert a sinner; a vindication of Christ; a petition for himself, which is full of confidence, and an implicit recognition of the kingship of Christ.

In lifting up us sinners to sanctity God is not hampered by the limitations of space and time. With a word He cured a man who had been ailing for thirty-six years and could do nothing to cope with his complaint. Here on Calvary as Dismas was being nailed to the cross, he uttered fearful oaths and blasphemies. Soon after he was speaking to Christ in a prayer full of reverence and deep sorrow. Circumstances of time and place cannot be an obstacle to impede God's action, to hinder Him when that moment comes which He has marked out for the offering of a special grace.

THIRD WORD: "Behold Your Son; Behold Your Mother"

I went into a Dublin office to discuss a project with the manager. When we had finished he told me about his son, a young man in his twenties, whom he had loved dearly. He had died four months before, and you never saw a brokenhearted man till you met his father. Presently he slipped his hand into his breast pocket and drew out a leather wallet. He told me to open it. It contained a small crucifix, a badge of the Sacred Heart, a medal of Our Lady. "Tom gave it to me," he explained, "half an hour before he died. I shall always treasure it — a parting gift, the last expression of his love for me."

There is something in our psychological makeup that makes us lay special stress on the significance and value of a parting gift. Christ knows this. He is lying on His deathbed, the hard bed of the cross, with a crown of thorns for His pillow. He forces His eyes open and looks down at Mary and John, the disciple whom He loved. To Mary He said, "Woman, behold your son," and to John: "Behold your mother." A parting gift of stupendous value. He had already given us one last night at the supper — the Eucharist, as His last will and testament. Now He adds a codicil to the will, naming Mary as our mother.

Our separated brethren think we read too much into these words. It seems to them that Jesus, now at the point of death, was simply asking John to take care of His mother. If this were so, one must think it strange that He should postpone such an important commission till the last moments of His life. Incidentally, Our Lady's presence on Calvary and Christ's obvious concern for her dispose of the theory that there was some estrangement between them, and it is claimed that this is supported by other texts. The commission to John also contradicts the insinuation, even still maintained in some contemporary writers, that Mary had other children.

Your Mother

The fact that Mary is our mother flows logically from the Incarnation. We are part of Christ's Mystical Body. He is head and we are members. St. Paul does not hesitate to use the daring words: "I live, but it is no longer I. It is Christ who is living in me." No woman is mother of only the head of her child. She is mother of the whole child, head and members, and we, in the splendid phrase of St. Augustine, make up with Jesus "the whole Christ." Some of the mystics say that we are "owned" with Christ. From this the truth is obvious that Mary is *our* mother.

A point not to miss is that Christ did not *constitute* Mary our mother on Calvary. She became His mother physically at the Incarnation and at the same moment mystically mother of the entire human race, as being "ones" with Him. All Jesus did on the cross was to *proclaim* what had already taken place.

The Church's liturgy, old and new, rings with the praises of Mary, Mother of God and man. Here are a few quotations from Vatican II. "Mary is hailed as a preeminent and altogether singular member of the Church and as the Church's model and excellent exemplar in faith and charity. Taught by the Holy Spirit the Catholic Church honors her with filial affection and piety as a most beloved mother."

Again. "In celebrating the annual cycle of Christ's mysteries, Holy Church honors, with special love, the Blessed Mary, Mother of God, who is joined by an inseparable bond to the saving work of her Son. In her the Church holds up and admires the most excellent fruit of our redemption, and joyfully contemplates, as in a faultless model, that which she (the Church) herself wholly desires and hopes to be." Finally, there is a timely warning against abuses. "The Church has endorsed many forms of piety towards the Mother of God, provided they were within the limits of sound and orthodox doctrine. ... It charges that practices and exercises of devotion towards her should be treasured ... and that those decrees issued in earlier times regarding the veneration of the images of Christ, the Blessed Virgin and the saints, be religiously observed. But this synod earnestly exhorts theologians and preachers, that, in treating of the unique dignity of the Mother of God, they carefully and equally avoid the falsity of exaggeration on the one hand and the excess of narrow-mindedness on the other."

The Popes Speak

Pope Pius XII solemnly consecrated the entire human race to Mary's Immaculate Heart. Pope Paul VI has proclaimed her Mother of the Church. He has given us an inspirational exhortation in which he dwells lovingly on her privileges and power, while insisting that our belief in them rests, not on mere sentiment, but on solid theological arguments.

There is much in this document we would wish to quote. It can be bought for a few pence and will repay many a careful reading. It is known as *Marialis Cultus* — in English, "To Honor Mary." Here is one particularly timely citation: "The picture of the Blessed Virgin presented in a certain type of devotional literature cannot easily be reconciled with today's life-style, especially with the way women live today in the home, woman's responsibility and equality with man in the running of the family are being justly recognized by laws and the evolution of customs. In the sphere of politics women have, in many countries, gained a position in public life equal to that of men. In the social field women are at work in a whole range of different employments, getting farther away every day from the restricted surroundings of the home. In the cultural field new possibilities are coming up for women in scientific research and intellectual activities.

"In consequence of these phenomena some people are becoming disenchanted with devotion to the Blessed Virgin, and finding it difficult to take as an example Mary of Nazareth, because the horizons of her life, so they say, seem rather restricted in comparison with the vast spheres of activity open to mankind today.

This is a real problem, which the Holy Father looks straight in the face. His solution is lengthy, and we can give only a few sentences indicative of the whole. "The modern woman," he writes, "will note with pleasant surprise, that Mary of Nazareth, while completely devoted to the Will of God, was far from being a timidly submissive woman or one whose piety was repellent to others. On the contrary she was a woman who did not hesitate to proclaim that God vindicates the humble and the oppressed . . . a woman of strength who experienced poverty and suffering, flight and exile.

"These are but examples, but examples which show clearly that the figure of the Blessed Virgin does not disillusion any of the profound expectations of the men and women of our time, but offers them the perfect model . . . the disciple who is the active witness of that love which builds up Christ in people's hearts. . . ."

Behold . . .

You cannot estimate the beauty or value of a gift until you take time to examine it. If it is a book you must read it. If it comes as a parcel in the mail you must remove the wrapping. If it is a clock or a fountain pen you must test it. This is what Jesus invites us to do as He gives us this parting gift. "Behold it," He says. "Look at it well and learn to appreciate it." When the angel Gabriel came to Mary at Nazareth and saw into the treasures in her soul, even he felt compelled to kneel before her in reverence and exclaim that she was full of grace. Angels had been sent on other occasions by God to man but they had always behaved as befitted someone of a higher nature — like Raphael, who guided Tobias through a long and difficult journey and gave him instructions which he clearly took for granted would be carried out.

But Gabriel does not presume to give orders to Mary. An angel is of a higher order of being than a human person, but this particular human person is unique. Suppose you could, somehow, gather together here around Mary the nine choirs of angels and all God's best friends from Old and New Testament, and if, like God, you could see the millions still to be born who will love and serve Him well; what a transcendently beautiful sight that would be!

But what do you discover when you "behold your mother"? Why, that in Mary's soul alone there is more of the love of God, more plenitude of grace, more zeal for souls, more personal sanctity, than in all the rest combined. Why is this? It is in God's Providence, whenever He calls someone to a special mission, to give to that person the graces and helps appropriate for the work He wants done. But Mary is unique. She stands on a pedestal all her own, because in the divine economy she is entrusted with an office in the light of which all other divinely-imposed tasks seem almost insignificant. And if Mary was already "full of grace" when Gabriel came, what a prodigy of grace must she have been by the time she was assumed into heaven! If she was "full of grace" at the Incarnation, her capacity to grow still more must have been continually on the increase as she lived through till she passed out of this world.

There is a motto: *De Maria nunquam satis;* "you can never feel satisfied that you have said enough about Mary." Thoughts keep flowing into our minds as often as we fulfill Our Lord's command to look well at her. An injunction, therefore, to carry out unceasingly. There are always new discoveries to be made.

Behold Your Son

There is often a family resemblance between a child and its parents. If Mary is our mother it is reasonable to expect that we should be like her. This likeness is principally in the interior. It develops, as it did in Mary, through the growth of grace — the communication of divine life — in our souls. This grace cones to us through contact with its source, which is Christ. But Christ comes through Mary. In one of the Church's official prayers she is spoken of as the one "through whom we have merited to receive *the Author of life.*" Hence she has a much stronger reason than St. Paul to say to us: "My little children, for whom I am in labor again, till Christ be fashioned in you." There are reputable Catholic writers who maintain that every grace we receive comes to us through the hands of Mary.

Our ideal is that Mary should be able to point to each of us and say to the eternal Father, "Behold Your son," or "Behold Your daughter." Through the grace she constantly infuses into our souls, the family resemblance becomes more and more sharply defined. We are, in a manner, divinized. Christ becomes "reincarnate in us."

FOURTH WORD: "My God, My God, Why Have You Forsaken Me?"

A brave woman tells me her story in a letter lying open before me. She had an ideal husband, kind and considerate and steady at his work, and a staunch Catholic. On December 23 he cycled five miles to get a few treats for the Christmas dinner. On his return he collapsed suddenly and died. Of course her heart was bleeding. It was a lonely Christmas. "Truly, Father, no one can understand a sorrow like this until it touches one's own heart. . . . But I am astonished at myself as I realize the strength and courage God has given me, and even peace and joy, under this heavy cross. I offer it to Him in reparation for my own sins, and the sins I see all around me — the hatred and murders and robberies, and abortions, the easy tolerance of sex sins, the neglect of Mass and the sacraments. . . .

"I see now the insanity of living merely for this world and what it can give. I am stricken with horror when I reflect on the selfishness of vices like marital infidelity and contraception, the fearful responsibility of the media which propagate them. Here in the silence of my empty home I am learning that I am not alone. . . . Each morning as I begin another day I am to take up my cross and walk with Jesus and Mary to Calvary. . . ."

This wonderful letter helps to provide the answer to the question contained in the fourth word of Christ on the cross. It is easy to persuade ourselves that we love God — and it is also probably quite true — when He sends us temporal blessings. We have everything we want, everything we need, not as much as a ripple on the surface of life's ocean to upset our calm. Thanks be to God! This is good, of course, but perhaps we have an uneasy feeling at times that this is armchair Christianity. The cross is notably absent. God sends it, but not because He is cruel. A surgeon who submits us to a painful operation is all out for our good. The divine physician sends the cross because, accepted in the right spirit, it will shrivel up the roots of selfishness. If even He, in whom there was no selfishness, had to suffer this feeling of forsakenness, how much more needed is the cross for us! This applies equally to mental anguish, loneliness, depression, fustration, which can often be more demanding than cancer or arthritis.

In Context

The first three words were spoken soon after Christ had been nailed and raised up on the cross. They were followed by a period of some two hours, which were passed in silence and in the gathering darkness. Then Christ, despite His complete exhaustion, sends out this cry, which is only a feeble expression of the reality of what He is suffering. "Forsaken!" This is grief of mind and heart that outweighs all the accumulation of pains inflicted on His body.

The setting is most appropriate for the message this fourth word is intended to convey. The tone of voice, the prolonged silence, the atmosphere charged with darkness and gloom, all help towards some appreciation of the reality f what He says. Hitherto, during the years behind Him, when He was insulted by men or ignored or contradicted or abandoned, He had always one unfailing support to sustain Him. He could always depend on the nearness of His heavenly Father. St. John refers to the Father one hundred and sixteen times as being the source of strength and consolation to His Son. Men might prove to be broken reeds, "yet I am not alone, because the Father is with me. . . ." But here on Calvary even this one support seems to give way. He exclaims that He has been "forsaken" and in His utter desolation He asks why.

Note that He says: "My God," not the more familiar form of address, "My Father."

This is indicative of the painful aloofness that seems to have come between them. Christ must, as we would say, keep His distance. And in what way was He "forsaken"? Many attempts have been made to answer this difficult question. A sentence from St. Paul suggests, perhaps, the most satisfactory explanation. "God," he writes, "spared not His own Son but delivered Him up for us all." The Father withdrew His protecting hand and permitted Christ's enemies to have their way. In this sense He forsook His Son.

"My God, My God, why have you forsaken me?" These are not words of accusation. They betray no indignation. They are not a complaint. Their object is, at least in part, to convince us that He really did feel His sufferings, mental and physical. Until now, throughout the whole Passion, He had borne His sufferings with such incredible patience and tranquillity that one might imagine He was insensible to them; that, perhaps by a miracle, He had preserved Himself from feeling pain. That such suppositions are groundless is clearly seen in this fourth word. Moreover, by uttering it "in a loud voice," He indicates how great was the price of our redemption.

"Consider," writes Newman, "that hardly any one stroke of pain is intolerable; it is intolerable when it continues. . . . The memory of the foregoing moments of pain acts upon us and, as it were, edges the pain that succeeds. . . . If the succession of the moments which preceded it could be forgotten, it would be no more than the first moment, as bearable as the first. . . . Christ drew back, at the proper moment, the bolts and fastenings and opened the gates, and the floods fell right upon Him in all their fullness. . . ."

Cooperation

St. Thérèse wrote that at one period of her life she felt God's presence so close to her that nothing seemed to come between except a thin veil, almost transparent. But a big change followed, and now it seemed as if a thick wall separated her from the God she loved, and, like Christ, she cried out that God had forsaken her.

He had not left her; He was closer than ever. All He did was take away the feeling, the conviction that He was there. This feeling of desolation comes invariably in all desirous of living a full Catholic life. Why? Briefly, in order to purify us of selfishness, the one obstacle to holiness of life, and to teach us experimentally that only God can help. "Give us help from your holy place, for the help that men can give is vain."

A Poor Clare writes: "God is hidden, absent, gone, and all light has gone out of life with Him. All brightness, interior and exterior, has faded away. No glamour is left. There is no sense of any 'beyond' but a chill finality checks all expectation. There seems to be nothing to hope for, nothing desirable. That which is beautiful has lost its enchantment, its inner meaning, its personal appeal, and the soul feels itself alone in the midst of all creation, tastes to the full what real loneliness is, for God is gone. . . . Thoughts suggested, sacred words, words which used to thrill, stimulating to great desires, high ideals, to love, joy and adoration, are now powerless. . . . They slip, so to say, over the soul's surface or leave no trace of their passage. . . ."

She is clearly writing from personal experience. This is the divine technique. When this dryness of spirit is not caused by one's own deliberate infidelity to grace, we can assume that it is sent by God and therefore it should not distress us unduly. When it has done its work of purification God will take it away and introduce the soul into deeper depths of "holy familiarity with God." In the exuberance of its joy it now realizes that all the preparatory work and desolation was a small price to pay for such unspeakable privilege.

FIFTH WORD: "I Thirst"

If you go visit a friend in the hospital after he has had a serious operation, he is morally certain to tell you all about his illness. Perhaps he will begin by describing the first symptoms, which appeared six months ago, and dwell on every detail that followed. Twenty minutes after you have gone another friend calls and your sick man tells the whole story all over again!

We do not want to censure him, but only to stress once more that contrast in the suffering Christ. "Jesus held His peace." The fifth word on the cross is the only direct reference He makes to His sufferings. What a marvelous subject for meditation this is! We feel compelled to repeat it in this context.

"I thirst." Why does He break His rule of silence here, for the first and only time? Not in order to get relief but "so that the scriptures might be fulfilled." Every detail, even down to the most minute, which the prophets told the Jews to look for by way of identifying the Messiah, had now been worked out before their eyes — all except one. The psalmist, speaking in the name of Christ, had written: "When I was thirsty they gave me vinegar to drink." Jesus knew that "now all things were accomplished" by which He would be recognizable, except this one remaining prophecy. A sponge was lying on the ground, used perhaps by the soldiers to wipe the blood off their arms and hands. One of them steeped it in vinegar, placed it on a stick about a foot long and held it to the lips of the dying Christ. He sipped a little from the sponge. Earlier in His life He had promised that "whoever shall give you to drink a cup of cold water in My name, I assure you solemnly that he will not lose his reward." Can we not assume, then, that He rewarded the soldier's act of charity, the last kindness shown to Him before He died?

He had asked the Samaritan woman for a drink of water, "the only time recorded in the gospel story when He asked anyone for anything."

Water

Had Jesus not called attention to His thirst, we might have overlooked it, and He was determined that not one single proof of the love He has for us should escape our notice. We can only guess at the intensity of the agony He suffered from this thirst. He had neither eaten nor drunk since the supper last night. He had lost a huge quantity of blood, especially in the scourging. One searched in vain for the words to express the torment this implies. When He wanted to bring home to us the reality of hell He stressed the consuming thirst of those who are lost. The rich man who "died and was buried in hell . . . looked up and saw Abraham, a long way off, with Lazarus in his bosom. So he cried out: 'Father Abraham, pity me and send Lazarus to dip the tip of his finger in water and cool my thirst, for I am in agony in these flames.' "

An alcoholic knocked at a convent door where lived a nun who was a friend of his. He told her he was nearly in despair. She was a woman of much experience and sound common sense. She encouraged him and advised him, and, before he left, she suggested he should kneel and take the pledge. As she was on the point of closing the hall door behind him, she said to him, slowly and very earnestly: "Surely, Tom, you can do that much for Christ, who bore the thirst of Calvary for you." That simple plan worked wonders. "Sometimes, Father, when I was nearly mad for a drink, I would force myself to slow down and repeat what Sister had told me. God bless her!"

Asking for More

When Jesus knelt in the garden last night He implored His Father not to ask Him drink the chalice. But now He speaks about His thirst, intimating that He no longer wants to refuse the chalice but rather to drain it to the dregs. Something like this seems to happen in the lives of those generous people who, aided by grace and not leaning themselves but on His divine strength, embark seriously on the way of the cross. At first it seems terrifying, as happened to Christ Himself, but, according as love deepens, there comes an insatiable longing to be like Him. Love of Him is henceforth supreme. Other loves there will be, but they will be the expression and the overflowing of the divine love, not an attempt to find a substitute for it. To it everything is subservient. "You shalt love the Lord your God with your *whole* heart, with your *whole* soul, with *all* your strength, with *all* your mind."

A mother was kneeling by the bedside of her dying son, a young man in his thirties. "Mother," he gasped, "the thirst is terrible; may I please have another drink?" Willingly she rose to get it for him. There it was in her left hand, a glass of sparkling cold water with a lump of ice floating on the surface. Everything that was in him seemed to crave for it. His mother, still holding the glass in her left hand, slipped her right arm around his frail body to help him to a sitting position. Just as she was in the act of bringing the drink to his burning lips, the clock in the kitchen downstairs struck three. "Did you hear that, Joe? Three o'clock and Friday afternoon, At this hour on Good Friday, Jesus, like you, was dying, and, like you, He was tortured with thirst." That was all she said. The poor lad looked longingly at the glass for a moment. Then, very deliberately, he raised his feeble left arm and pushed it aside untouched. A brave lad, but a braver woman. All her motherly instincts urged her to give him relief. Why did she not do so?

I told that story in a retreat. A mother came to me afterwards and said she could not agree. Had that mother I described really loved her son she would never have withheld from him what he longed for. Perhaps that is at least debatable. But I cannot forget that when Mary heard that cry from her dying son she had to continue standing there, helpless to do anything about it.

A Loud Voice

Here is St. Paul's summary of the mystery of the cross: "Here we are, preaching a crucified Christ; to the Jews an obstacle they cannot get over and to the gentiles madness, but to those who have been called, whether they be Jews or Greeks, a Christ who is the power of God and the wisdom of God. For God's foolishness is wiser than human reason and God's weakness is stronger than human strength" (I Cor. 1:3-25).

Another reason might be suggested why Christ called attention to His thirst. His throat was parched and His tongue dry. He had still a final message to deliver to the world. This would be contained in His sixth and seventh words from the cross. Humanly speaking, it would have been impossible for Him to give utterance to it, above all "with a loud voice" as He wanted to do, unless His tongue was moistened. Public speakers generally have a glass of water on a table close to them. They sit from it from time to time so as to be able to put more force and emphasis into what they have to say. What Christ had still to convey to us was of supreme importance. Because He wanted to say it in the most effective manner, He said He was thirsty, implying that He wished to drink. We often remind ourselves that Christ *died* on the cross. It is well to remember that He also *lived* on the cross for three terrible hours.

On my desk I always keep a photo of a poor Vietnamese woman. She is starving, and the little sick baby at her breast is diseased and dying. It helps me to remember the millions who are "filling up in their flesh the things that are wanting to the sufferings of Christ." Suffering is a mystery but this much at least we can understand — that it produces saints, and that through these suffering people Christ continues to say to us: "I thirst."

SIXTH WORD: "It Is Consummated"

Humanly speaking, Calvary was the most ignominious failure ever. Christ's enemies had everything their own way. They had left nothing undone which hatred and contempt could devise to multiply the mental and bodily sufferings of their victim. They stand here on this hillside watching Him as he enters on the final stage of His Passion. Surely they will relent a little, at least before He dies. Surely there must be left in their hearts some remnants of humanity, prompting them to say a word of sympathy — since anything more is impossible at this stage — for the innocent man whom they have treated so brutally. This might be expected even if they believed Him to be indeed a criminal and even if He was, in fact, all they thought Him to be. Guilty or not guilty, He is now at the point of death. Guilty or not guilty, He has waded through a sea of blood. Will not even shame or remorse compel them to show some small gesture of sympathy? In fact they are witnessing His last moments from a very different angle. These they regard as their own last opportunity to hurl taunts and insults at Christ. They stand there in front of Him and point at Him the finger of scorn. They defy Him to come down from the cross if He can. They are jubilant to observe that seemingly He cannot accept the challenge. "He saved others; himself he cannot save." Their mockeries are a shout of victory. Christ is a failure, a dreamer of dreams, a fanatic, a fool.

Consummation

"Consummation" means, in the first place, that the final touches have been put to a piece of work. The author lays down his pen. The artist rises from his stool, stands back to view his picture, and tells himself it is as perfect as he can make it. This is how the Jews regard their work on Calvary. "It is consummated." Their hatred has torn Him in pieces. It is not sated but it is "consummated," in the sense that it has searched up and down every avenue to see if it can discover any further instruments of torture. It finds none. There are none left. It has employed all of them.

"It is consummated." Calvary is with us today, and today men are exercising their minds to discover means by which to show their contempt for Christ, their hatred, and the diabolical skill with which they seek to make Him suffer in the members of the Church, His Mystical Body. We illustrated this a few pages back when we set out some facts concerning Blessed Maximilian Kolbe. This entire book could be filled with similar stories. It is impossible to exaggerate the degree of hatred of Christ at which we have arrived in this century. He has not only avowed enemies outside who make open profession of their feelings toward Him. He has traitors within the camp who, Judas-like, pose as His friends but betray Him with a kiss. Their hate is consummated but not sated; their boast is that it is only a matter of time till Catholicism is wiped off the map, or at least barely surviving in dark catacombs.

By no means can we brush these threats aside as vain mouthings. It is beyond question that the Church, like Christ, is bleeding on the cross from many wounds, and it is easy to understand why those who oppose her are convinced that she will — at last — bleed to death.

But "consummation" on the lips of Our Lord means also and especially a shout of victory. His sufferings are "consummated," and He has won, despite appearances. "Where, O death, is your victory? Where, O death, is your sting? . . . So let us thank God for giving us the victory through Our Lord Jesus Christ. Never give in then, my dear brothers, never admit defeat; keep on working at the Lord's work always, knowing that, in the Lord, you cannot be laboring in vain" (1 Cor. 15:55-58). He tells us, too, how to turn the seeming failure of Calvary into a magnificent success. "[Do not] go on living the aimless kind of life that pagans live. Intellectually they are in the dark, and they are estranged from the life of God, without knowledge because they have shut their hearts to it. . . . So be very careful about the sort of lives you live, like intelligent, and not like senseless people. This may be a wicked age but your lives should redeem it. *Be like children of light.* The effects of the light are seen in complete goodness and right living and truth" (Ephesians 4:17-18; 5:15-16, 8-9).

A Consecrated Life

When we speak about a man whose life was consecrated to science or art, we imply that he was so absorbed by science or art that he thought of nothing else. A vessel is consecrated — a chalice, for example — when it is set aside for one only purpose, the service of the altar. If a church is consecrated it may never be lawfully used for any purpose other than what directly concerns the worship of God.

It is reasonable to suppose that when Christ said "it is consummated," He spoke of the life He had lived, which was now fast ending. When we look back with Him over the years behind, what do we find? A life of most consistent and complete consecration to the will of His Father. "I came down from heaven," He declared, "not to do my own will but the will of him who sent me" (John 6:38). Never once had He swerved an inch from that principle, to left or right. Whether He lived in Nazareth or Jerusalem; whether He fasted or took food; whether He prayed or preached; whether He slept or remained awake; whether He spoke or kept silence — in all He was governed completely by the will of the Father and the guidance of His Holy Spirit. And now that the end has come He says His great "Amen" to that consecrated life which is consummated.

What this means for ourselves is admirably explained by the

late Archbishop Goodier. "To have as little as possible to do with the making of my own career. What God wills, let it be done by me. To be ready, as far as I may, for anything and everything. For this, to make the best of myself, so far as opportunity allows. There will always be something wrong, always there will be something to be done. To do the duty of each day as it comes, for its own sake, because it is a duty, the gift of God to me, not looking too much into the future, not looking too much for results. Fidelity in the present spells fidelity in the future.

"To know that God, almighty and all-loving, is behind all, with His hand on every thread, personally interested in all things, in me, in His own great design, in that portion of it for which He has particularly made me. To trust Him blindly, knowing that His wisdom is more comprehensive than mine, His goal different from, grander than mine, His ways not as my ways but infinitely more sure.

"To recognize this again and again in my everyday experience; *how underneath seeming failure* success is constantly attained — my failure His success; of another kind, it may be, from what I had anticipated, but in the end far more real and important. To see how, in an instant, He restores or replaces what seems utterly to have collapsed; how for all the ends He has in view the means are always found."

This is the consecrated life. Happy the soul who can say "it is consummated" when the end comes!

Success and failure are very different things according as they are weighted in the scales of man or the scales of God. The world, by and large, estimates success by what a man *has;* Christ by what a man *is.* Dives, as his very name suggests, had plenty of money; he dined and wined well seven days of the week; he had security himself, and it did not even occur to him to help Lazarus, the poor beggarman covered with sores, starving and shivering with cold at his gate. Which of the two was a success, and which was the failure? When one sits back and reflects prayerfully, as we are doing while reading this book, we cannot but be amazed and made sorrowful at the blindness and folly of so many men who are counted as wise, but in reality are fools. All the time and energy "consumed" in the struggle for power, for more money, for position, for popularity, "the fascination of trifles!" So mesmerized by what we see and hear and feel and eat and wear that there is no time left to pause and try to grasp the truth that "we have not here a lasting city but seek one that is to come." This is not jargon or pious twaddle. It is the realism confronting every man who views life whole, not only in the present fleeting state but when "it is consummated."

This sixth word is a cry of joy, of gratitude, of relief. All through His life Christ had looked forward with dread to His sufferings and death. These He had foretold in great detail to His disciples. "Now we are going up to Jerusalem, and the Son of Man is about to be handed over to the chief priests and the scribes. They will condemn him to death and will hand him over to the pagans to be mocked and scourged and crucified; and on the third day he will rise again" (Mark 9:30). All that He shrank from in terror is now behind Him and this sixth word is a shout of victory, proclaiming the triumph of failure.

We cannot refrain from quoting one of St. Paul's many inspiring texts. It is a perfect summary of the contents of Our Lord's sixth word. He writes to his disciple Timothy: "As for me, my life is already being poured out like a libation, and the time has come for me to be gone. I have fought the good fight to the end. I have run the race to the finish. I have kept the faith. All that there is to come now is the crown of righteousness reserved for me, which the Lord, the righteous judge, will give me on that day — *and not only to me*, but to all who have longed for his coming" (2 Timothy 4:6-8).

Cardinal Wright, in his book *Words in Pain*, has this to say: "Those who have lived with indifference to God's grace generally take leave of life in that same disposition of indifference. . . . Those who have lived preoccupied with self and property, with the little world they have built for themselves, go into eternity with a backward glance, eyes fixed hungrily upon the shore that is fading from sight. . . .

"On the heartening side, however, the man who has been accustomed through life to walk constantly in the presence of God, who has sincerely striven ever to do all things in God, and through God, and unto God, whose prayer has been "Thy kingdom come" — such a one is already directed toward heaven, and the transition from earth to paradise is almost incidental.

"For him there will be, there need be, no final frantic turn to God as the end approaches. He will conclude his life just as he would close a favorite book, turn down the light and climb the stairs. With him there will be no startled cry, no stupefaction. He will be perfectly at home with God, hereafter as here below. He will arrive already part of heaven and with heaven already part of him."

SEVENTH WORD: "Father, Into Your Hands I Commend My Spirit"

A cousin of mine bought a ticket to travel by plane to Lourdes with her sister. Ten days before the departure she got cold feet and cancelled the trip. There is always the risk. Whether we embark on a journey by air or by sea or by land; whether we go by bus or train or car or plane, we are committing ourselves, probably without adverting to the fact, into the hands of the pilot or driver. We know nothing about him. We assume he has passed all the tests, that he is conscientious and sober and fully alive to the responsibility he is undertaking. Just the same, men in this position, generally through no fault of their own, have lost control of the machine and ended in fearful disaster.

Life is a journey from time into eternity. It is fraught with dangers. We could have a head-on crash. We may be held up at the point of a gun. In these appalling times, when human blood is cheap, when even men who call themselves Christians arrogate to themselves God's inalienable right over life and death, we could be killed in an explosion or murdered in cold blood. There are moral dangers too. Because these contain a germ which could jeopardize our eternal salvation, they are the most terrible menace of all. They are known as the world, the flesh and the devil. The world is an infected area, and it is easy to inhale into our lungs the poisoned air with which the atmosphere is charged. There is Satan, who is no harmless clown in cap and bells but a fierce monster, an accomplished psychologist, an unscrupulous liar, with vast experience in dealing with the human race since time began. Poor St. John is dated. "The love of the Father," he writes, "cannot be in any man who loves the world, because nothing that the world has to offer — the sensual body, the lust-

238

ful eye, pride in possessions — could ever come from the Father but only from the world" (1 John 2:16). Satan and the world are outside of us. There is, further, our own concupiscence. "I am delighted," said St. Paul, "with the law of God according to the inner man. But I see another law in my members, fighting against the law of my mind and captivating me by the law of sin which is in my members. Unhappy man that I am, who will deliver me from the body of this death?" (Romans 7:22-24).

The Answer

The answer to the apostle's question is implied in Christ's last word on the cross. "Into your hands, O Father, I commend My spirit." This sentence is from the Thirty-first Psalm with which Christ would have been familiar. Possibly Mary, like many a good mother since, would have said it with him as she put him to bed. "Ever since the sacrifice on Golgotha, "writes Msgr. O'Rahilly, "millions have laid their suffering and death beside that of the Son of God; trusting that, in spite of seeming failure, their lives will in the end be finished in His sight, and that their souls will be committed to our Father in heaven."

So this last word of Christ reminds us that we have a trustworthy guide, not only when we are drawing near the end of life but in every phase through which we pass along the route. "The Lord is my light and my salvation; whom shall I fear?" Of course temptations will rise up in our path. Of course we have crafty enemies to deal with. Of course we make mistakes and commit sin. But here is Christ teaching us to cast all our care on Him for He has care of us. Everything is under control in His hands. "The souls of the just are in the hands of God."

The story of Tobias or Tobiah from the Old Testament fits in here. He had a long and difficult journey to make and he did not know the way. He was on the lookout for someone to direct him, and one day he encountered a young man like himself, a stranger. In the course of their conversation Tobias asked him if he happened to know the road to Media, the country he wanted to visit. "Certainly I do," came the answer. "I have been there many times. I know the way by heart." "Wait for me, friend," said Tobias, "while I go and tell my father. I need you to come with me and I will pay you for your time." "Good," said the other. "I will wait, but do not be long." Tobias set out and learned that his guide was as good as his word. He took complete charge, knew how to cope with difficulties, gave wise advice, and, when they two had completed their tasks in Media, the stranger conducted his charge back home to his father.

It was only then that he revealed his identity. "I am Raphael," he told them, "one of the seven angels who stand ever ready to enter the presence of the glory of God. . . . Now bless the Lord on earth and give thanks to God. I am about to return to Him Who sent me."

Newman

Newman tells a similar story in his poem "The Dream of Gerontius." Gerontius is first shown to us at the point of death. When his soul leaves the body it is clasped in the arms of his angel guardian and borne in flight to the throne of God. There is much one would wish to quote but we have to skip until we reach the last stanza. The angel leads Gerontius to purgatory, and Newman puts these parting words on the lips of his guide:

> "Softly and gently, dearly-ransomed soul,
> In my most loving arms I now enfold thee.
> And o'er the penal waters as they roll
> I poise thee, and I lower thee, and hold thee.
>
> And carefully I dip thee in the lake,
> And thou, without a sob or a resistance

Dost through the flood thy rapid passage take,
Sinking deep, deeper, into the dim distance.

Angels to whom the willing task is given,
Shall tend and nurse and lull thee as thou liest;
And Masses on the earth and prayer in heaven
Shall aid thee at the throne of the Most Highest.

Farewell, but not forever, brother dear.
Be brave and patient on thy bed of sorrow;
Swiftly shall pass thy night of trial here,
And I will come and wake thee on the morrow."

Like Tobias, like Gerontius, we too have each an angel to guide us. "God has given his angels charge over you, and in their hands they bear you up, lest you dash your foot against a stone" (Psalm 91:11-12). This is high privilege, but the seventh word reminds us that there is one higher still. For the angels are only His agents, His delegates to carry out the commission entrusted to them by Him. They too are under His control, and the fidelity and eagerness with which they take care of us reflect the love for us implied in the orders He has given them concerning us. You will not put a hundred gold coins (if you had them) into the hands of a child to keep for you. You will look for someone with a sense of responsibility. The fact that our Father would give to angels only the care of each one of us is, in itself, a clear indication of the value He sets upon us.

He keeps, so to say, a watching brief over them all through our lives, and when we reach the end, and when we have commended our spirit into His hands, He gives us the thrilling assurance that "no one can snatch them out of the hand of my Father"!

And we, for our part, will exclaim: "I have found him whom my soul loves; I have held him fast and will never let him go." All this is no mere pleasing fantasy. It is as factual as what

St. John tells us in his first epistle. "This is what we have heard from him and the message that we are announcing to you. God is light; there is no darkness in him at all." We have written this book as a help to a "real" assent as opposed to a "notional" one to these dynamic truths.

Father Daniel Lord, S.J.

Father Lord was an American Jesuit who died in the States about forty years ago. He died of cancer in both lungs. His whole life was dedicated unreservedly to the apostolate, but most of all his last few months on earth are an inspiring commentary on the seventh word of Christ on the cross. "This spiritual giant," to quote his colleague, Father Gavin, "rose, or rather soared, above the most dreaded of human maladies." On learning the doctor's verdict, far from sinking down into inactivity and coddling himself, on the contrary Father Lord felt in his bones that this report was a new challenge to him from Christ. He must seize upon this, the last chance he ever would have, to further the interests of the Master he had served with unflagging energy for more than half a century. He began by writing an essay, which was printed thousands of times and circulated all over America and Canada. This will not surprise you when you read even an extract. Here it is, and I do not think any normal person can reflect on it without deep emotion. "When the verdict was cancer I was relieved," he tells us. "I had expected to die some day of heart trouble or a stroke, and I dreaded the suddenness and, perhaps, sacramentless death. Cancer seemed kindly. I liked the gentle warning. In a sudden spurt of energy and determination to use time to the best advantage, I found I was itching to be at my typewriter to write some of the books I had long planned. I hit the road, back to my routine of talks and meetings and play rehearsals. So often have I taught the faith to others, that, of a sudden, I found my friend cancer teaching the faith to me. The realization that one has cancer sharpens one's whole outlook on life. The earth is more beautiful, the sky a little clearer, and every minute of the day precious, a thing to be hoarded." During the few months that followed, this incredible man addressed thousands of people in nine different states, wrote, produced and directed two mammoth plays, gave several retreats, preached the "Three Hours" on Good Friday, and wrote at least one full-length book. When finally he went to hospital to die, his cheerfulness and serenity astonished all who met him. The secret of the immense peace of his soul was that he had sounded the depths of Christ's prayer and had learned to say: "Father, into Your hands I commend my spirit."

Of the many pamphlets written by Father Lord there is one called "Death Isn't Terrible." True, but in his case gross understatement. "I reckon that the sufferings of this present time are not worthy to be compared to the glory to come, which will be revealed in us. . . . For that which is at present light and momentary of our tribulation, worketh for us, *beyond measure exceedingly*, an eternal weight of glory." In view of this, how could death, by any stretching of the imagination, be thought of as "terrible"?

Father Lord, occupied with his Father's business, made many a trip by land and sea and air. I do not know if he had any accidents. But this at least we may assume — that he reached the final station safely, under the expert guidance of the heavenly Father, into whose hands he had commended his soul. Mary, Mother of Jesus, was also there to welcome him home. Had he not begged her, thousands of times over, to pray for him, "now and at the hour of my death"?

"Precious in the sight of the Lord is the death of his saints."

EPILOGUE

EPILOGUE

Christ never spoke of His Passion without reminding His hearers that it would be followed by the Resurrection. "Now we are going up to Jerusalem, and everything that is written in the prophets about the Son of Man is to come true. For he will be handed over to the pagans and will be mocked and maltreated and spat upon, and when they have scourged him they will put him to death; and on the third day he will rise again" (Luke 18:31-33). Something similar would happen to themselves. "I tell you most solemnly you will be weeping and wailing while the world will rejoice; you will be made sorrowful, but your sorrow will turn into joy. A woman in childbirth suffers because her time is come. But when she has given birth to the child, she forgets her suffering in her joy that a man has been born into the world. So it is with you. You are sad now. But I shall see you again, and your hearts will be full of joy, and that joy no man shall take from you" (John 16:20-22).

This is the theme we propose in our epilogue. It almost writes itself, for it is stressed many times in both Old and New Testaments. "Do not abandon yourself to sorrow," Ecclesiasticus advises. "Beguile your cares. Do not torment yourself with brooding. Gladness of heart is life to a man; joy is what gives him length of days. Console your heart. Chase sorrow far away, for sorrow has been the ruin of many and is no use to anybody" (Sirach 30:22-25).

Christ speaks constantly in this strain. At the last supper He warned His friends: "Let not your heart be troubled nor let it be afraid. Trust in God still and trust in me. . . . I am going now to prepare a place for you, and after I have gone and prepared you a place, I shall return to take you with me, so that where I am, you may be also."

There was nobody who absorbed this teaching into his mind and heart as fully as St. Paul. Here is what we find as we turn over the pages of his letters, almost at random. "What the Spirit brings is . . . love, joy, patience, kindness, goodness, trustfulness, gentleness and self-control" (Galatians 5:22-23). "I want you to be happy," he assures the Philippians, "always happy in the Lord. I repeat — what I want is your happiness . . . that peace of God which is so much greater than we can understand will guard your hearts and your thoughts in Christ Jesus" (4:4-7).

"Constantly traveling, I have been in danger from rivers and in danger from brigands; in danger from my own people and in danger from pagans; in danger in the town; in danger in the country . . . often without sleep . . . hungry and thirsty and often starving. . . ." Is he depressed? Not he. "In all our trouble," he tells them again, "I am filled with consolation and my joy is overflowing." For Christ Calvary was not the end, only the beginning, and it was this conviction that sustained His faithful disciple. If we suffer with Him, we shall also surely rejoice with Him.

Emmaus

On the evening of the first Easter Sunday Christ overtook two men who were walking together along a country road. A wonderful episode followed, which we are strongly recommended to read prayerfully in St. Luke's twenty-fourth chapter. For our present purpose the keyword is *sperabamus*. "We had high hopes," they told Him, "but they are all dashed to the ground."

Before going on with the story let me pause to quote a few sentences from a priest friend of mind. "I certainly do not go along with those," he tells me, "who would describe the present crisis in the Church as an oversized storm in a teacup. But it can never measure up to the woeful situations witnessed in the fourth century, when, several times, heresy within and paganism without threatened to undermine every Christian community. Nor can it measure up to the pre-Reformation crisis, when both papacy and episcopacy, not to mention religious life, were, for the most part, as contradictory to the precepts of the sermon on the mount and the last supper discourse as they could well be.

"I see too much good in the Church at the moment, being done, not by the advocates of crisis, but by the hopeful leaven of the mass ... a great individual and group aspiration to pray — I'm not blind to the dangers of the charismatic movement — great idealism among the young, great concern for social justice. I see all these, and much more of the same kind, side by side with the huge clumps of darnel. . . ."

He goes on to take issue with persons who present us consistently with a picture of the contemporary Church that is all shadow and darkness and scarcely relieved by a single ray of light. He compares such writers to the "heresy-hunters" of another age, and I suspect he has in mind too the "prophets of doom," censured by Pope John. Certainly they have very distressing stories to tell, the reading of which, I confess, has often caused me anguish and tempted me to think, like the two men on the first Easter day, that the Church is faced with a situation, which, humanly speaking, is hopeless. *Sperabamus!*

On that eventful evening the Light of the World was walking beside them, and they could not see! He was alive and risen when they thought He was still buried and sleeping the sleep of death. Their hearts were crushed. Their eyes were held. They were soured, disappointed, disillusioned men, for whom life had become a blind alley. Looking at the whole episode in retrospect, as we are able to do, we find ourselves heartened by their obvious love for Christ, while we have to deplore their sadness and frustration. Christ Himself told them they were "foolish and slow of heart to believe." Why did they not remember that He had warned them about the harrowing details of His forthcoming Passion, but never without stressing the fact that it would be followed by the joys of resurrection?

Prophets of Doom?

We have to admit that Christ Himself was "a prophet of doom." To be convinced of this we have only to recall His stern condemnation of pharisees and scribes, and His warning that Jerusalem would collapse so completely that not a stone would remain upon a stone. In our own day Our Lady, too, has appeared repeatedly, and uttered dire "prophecies of forthcoming doom," unless men repent of their crimes. By no means are we permitted to bury our heads in the sand like the ostrich and try to pretend that the Church never had it better. We are agonizingly aware of those "huge clumps of darnel." But what we must deprecate is the tendency to concentrate so exclusively on the scandals and abuses as to create the impression that these constitute the entire story. "It is better to light a candle — or even strike a match — than curse the darkness."

This lopsidedness injures, in the first place, the person who adopts it. "All things are yellow to the jaundiced eye." He can easily develop a frame of mind that is harsh, sarcastic, self-opinionated, and devoid of a saving sense of humor. In the extreme case he might come to regard himself as an unappreciated martyr! He could develop a stubbornness and obstinacy he thinks is indicative of strong willpower, but his friends, if they dared, would like to suggest it might be no more than a smokescreen behind which lurks a hidden pride. All this must affect his own spiritual life adversely, possibly even disastrously.

An outstanding example of this calamity is the Dominican Friar Savonarola. Newman incorporates the sad story, in masterly fashion, into his essay on St. Philip Neri. It is possible to give here only a thumbnail summary.

Savonarola burned with zeal for God's glory and with fury and indignation for the scandals rampant in the Church.

He lashed out with fearful invective against pope and peasant. He fasted and prayed and scourged his body. A born orator, when he stepped into his pulpit in the Dominican Church in Florence, he electrified his hearers. They came from everywhere, huge congregations, hanging on his words, going home smitten with shame and sorrow. He transformed Florence so completely that the city of sin became a sanctuary, but there was woeful anticlimax, due, one suspects, to the fact that there was too much Savonarola in the preacher and not enough of the charity of Jesus Christ. This priest, with so many sterling qualities, ended by being hanged and burned to death; the blaze of conversions soon died down, and the city and citizens forgot even the fact that a great prophet had once walked among them.

The dark image of the Church, unrelieved by any glimmer of light, can also damage the spiritual lives of the persons to whom it is presented. They become querulous, unsettled, impetuous, ready at a moment's notice to rant and serve up the latest piece of spicy scandal, and to open fire on any who do not share their views. The Apostles John and James wanted to do just this, when the hostile Samaritans refused to give Christ a night's lodging. They were told by Him: "You do not know of what spirit you are." Would He have said the same to Savonarola? And, maybe, also to those who refuse to light a candle or even strike a match to dispel at least a fraction of the surrounding darkness?

"I have but one desire — Jesus.
One fear — to lose Jesus.
One to rest on — Jesus.
One home — the wounds of Jesus.
One occupation — to converse with Jesus.
One charge — to do the Will of Jesus.

One joy — to possess Jesus.
One hope — to see Jesus.
One grief — compassion for Jesus.
One witness — the eye of Jesus.
One consolation — to suffer for Jesus.
One glory — to be despised for Jesus.
One rest — to labor for Jesus.
One refuge — the heart of Jesus."